THE GOSPEL OF JOHN

THE IGNATIUS CATHOLIC STUDY BIBLE

REVISED STANDARD VERSION
SECOND CATHOLIC EDITION

THE GOSPEL OF JOHN

With Introduction, Commentary, and Notes

by

Scott Hahn and Curtis Mitch

and

with Study Questions by

Dennis Walters

IGNATIUS PRESS   SAN FRANCISCO

Published with ecclesiastical approval.

Original RSV Bible text:
Nihil obstat: Thomas Hanlon, S.T.L., L.S.S., Ph.L.
Imprimatur: +Peter W. Bertholome, D.D.
Bishop of Saint Cloud, Minnesota
May 11, 1966

Second Catholic Edition approved under the same *imprimatur* by the
Secretariat for Doctrine and Pastoral Practices,
National Conference of Catholic Bishops
February 29, 2001

Introduction, commentaries, and notes:
Nihil obstat: Rev. Msgr. J. Warren Holleran, S.T.D.
Imprimatur: + William J. Levada,
Archbishop of San Francisco,
December 5, 2002

The *nihil obstat* and *imprimatur* are official declarations that a book or pamphlet is free of doctrinal or moral error. No implication is contained therein that those who have granted the *nihil obstat* and *imprimatur* agree with the contents, opinions, or statements expressed.

Cover art: *John the Evangelist on Patmos*
Hans Burgmair the Elder, Alte Pinakothek, Munich
Scala/Art Resource, N.Y.

Cover design by Riz Boncan Marsella

Published for Ignatius Press in 2003 by
Thomas Nelson Publishers, Nashville, Tennessee

CONTENTS

INTRODUCTION TO THE IGNATIUS STUDY BIBLE

You are approaching the "word of God". This is the title Christians most commonly give to the Bible, and the expression is rich in meaning. It is also the title given to the Second Person of the Blessed Trinity, God the Son. For Jesus Christ became flesh for our salvation, and "the name by which he is called is The Word of God" (Rev 19:13; cf. Jn 1:14).

The word of God is Scripture. The Word of God is Jesus. This close association between God's *written* word and his *eternal* Word is intentional and has been the custom of the Church since the first generation. "All Sacred Scripture is but one book, and this one book is Christ, 'because all divine Scripture speaks of Christ, and all divine Scripture is fulfilled in Christ'[1]" (CCC 134). This does not mean that the Scriptures are divine in the same way that Jesus is divine. They are, rather, divinely inspired and, as such, are unique in world literature, just as the Incarnation of the eternal Word is unique in human history.

Yet we can say that the inspired word resembles the incarnate Word in several important ways. Jesus Christ is the Word of God incarnate. In his humanity, he is like us in all things, except for sin. As a work of man, the Bible is like any other book, except without error. Both Christ and Scripture, says the Second Vatican Council, are given "for the sake of our salvation" (*Dei Verbum* 11), and both give us God's definitive revelation of himself. We cannot, therefore, conceive of one without the other: the Bible without Jesus, or Jesus without the Bible. Each is the interpretive key to the other. And because Christ is the subject of all the Scriptures, St. Jerome insists, "Ignorance of the Scriptures is ignorance of Christ"[2] (CCC 133).

When we approach the Bible, then, we approach Jesus, the Word of God; and in order to encounter Jesus, we must approach him in a prayerful study of the inspired word of God, the Sacred Scriptures.

Inspiration and Inerrancy   The Catholic Church makes mighty claims for the Bible, and our acceptance of those claims is essential if we are to read the Scriptures and apply them to our lives as the Church intends. So it is not enough merely to nod at words like "inspired", "unique", or "inerrant". We have to understand what the Church means by these terms, and we have to make that understanding our own. After all, what we believe about the Bible will inevitably influence the way we read the Bible. The way we read the Bible, in turn, will determine what we "get out" of its sacred pages.

These principles hold true no matter what we read: a news report, a search warrant, an advertisement, a paycheck, a doctor's prescription, an eviction notice. How (or whether) we read these things depends largely upon our preconceived notions about the reliability and authority of their sources—and the potential they have for affecting our lives. In some cases, to misunderstand a document's authority can lead to dire consequences. In others, it can keep us from enjoying rewards that are rightfully ours. In the case of the Bible, both the rewards and the consequences involved take on an ultimate value.

What does the Church mean, then, when she affirms the words of St. Paul: "All Scripture is inspired by God" (2 Tim 3:16)? Since the term "inspired" in this passage could be translated "God-breathed", it follows that God breathed forth his word in the Scriptures as you and I breathe forth air when we speak. This means that God is the primary author of the Bible. He certainly employed human authors in this task as well, but he did not merely assist them while they wrote or subsequently approve what they had written. God the Holy Spirit is the *principal* author of Scripture, while the human writers are *instrumental* authors. These human authors freely wrote everything, and only those things, that God wanted: the word of God in the very words of God. This miracle of dual authorship extends to the whole of Scripture, and to every one of its parts, so that whatever the human authors affirm, God likewise affirms through their words.

The principle of biblical inerrancy follows logically from this principle of divine authorship. After all, God cannot lie, and he cannot make mistakes. Since the Bible is divinely inspired, it must be without error in everything that its divine and human authors affirm to be true. This means that biblical inerrancy is a mystery even broader in scope than infallibility, which guarantees for us that the Church will always teach the truth concerning faith and morals. Of course the mantle of inerrancy likewise covers faith and morals, but it extends even farther to ensure that all the facts and events of salvation history are accurately presented for us in the Scriptures. Inerrancy is our guarantee that the words and deeds of God found in the Bible are unified and true, declaring with one voice the wonders of his saving love.

---

[1] Hugh of St. Victor, *De arca Noe* 2, 8: PL 176, 642: cf. ibid. 2, 9: PL 176, 642–43.
[2] *DV* 25; cf. Phil 3:8 and St. Jerome, *Commentariorum Isaiam libri xviii*, prol.: PL 24, 17b.

The guarantee of inerrancy does not mean, however, that the Bible is an all-purpose encyclopedia of information covering every field of study. The Bible is not, for example, a textbook in the empirical sciences, and it should not be treated as one. When biblical authors relate facts of the natural order, we can be sure they are speaking in a purely descriptive and "phenomenological" way, according to the way things appeared to their senses.

Biblical Authority Implicit in these doctrines is God's desire to make himself known to the world and to enter a loving relationship with every man, woman, and child he has created. God gave us the Scriptures not just to inform or motivate us; more than anything he wants to save us. This higher purpose underlies every page of the Bible, indeed every word of it.

In order to reveal himself, God used what theologians call "accommodation". Sometimes the Lord stoops down to communicate by "condescension"—that is, he speaks as humans speak, as if he had the same passions and weakness that we do (for example, God says he was "sorry" that he made man in Genesis 6:6). Other times he communicates by "elevation"—that is, by endowing human words with divine power (for example, through the prophets). The numerous examples of divine accommodation in the Bible are an expression of God's wise and fatherly ways. For a sensitive father can speak with his children either by condescension, as in baby talk, or by elevation, by bringing a child's understanding up to a more mature level.

God's word is thus saving, fatherly, and personal. Because it speaks directly to us, we must never be indifferent to its content; after all, the word of God is at once the object, cause, and support of our faith. It is, in fact, a test of our faith, since we see in the Scriptures only what faith disposes us to see. If we believe what the Church believes, we will see in Scripture the saving, inerrant, and divinely authored revelation of the Father. If we believe otherwise, we see another book altogether.

This test applies not only to rank-and-file believers but also to the Church's theologians and hierarchy, and even the Magisterium. Vatican II has stressed in recent times that Scripture must be "the very soul of sacred theology" (*Dei Verbum* 24). Joseph Cardinal Ratzinger echoes this powerful teaching with his own, insisting that, "The *normative theologians* are the authors of Holy Scripture" [emphasis added]. Elsewhere he reminds us that Scripture and the Church's dogmatic teaching are tied tightly together, to the point of being inseparable. He states: "Dogma is by definition nothing other than an interpretation of Scripture." The defined dogmas of our faith, then, encapsulate the Church's infallible interpretation of Scripture, and theology is a further reflection upon that work.

The Senses of Scripture Because the Bible has both divine and human authors, we are required to master a different sort of reading than we are used to. First, we must read Scripture according to its *literal* sense, as we read any other human literature. At this initial stage, we strive to discover the meaning of the words and expressions used by the biblical writers as they were understood in their original setting and by their original recipients. This means, among other things, that we do not interpret everything we read "literalistically", as though Scripture never speaks in a figurative or symbolic way (it often does!). Rather, we read it according to the rules that govern its different literary forms of writing, depending on whether we are reading a narrative, a poem, a letter, a parable, or an apocalyptic vision. The Church calls us to read the divine books in this way to ensure that we understand what the human authors were laboring to explain to God's people.

The literal sense, however, is not the only sense of Scripture, since we interpret its sacred pages according to the *spiritual* senses as well. In this way, we search out what the Holy Spirit is trying to tell us, beyond even what the human authors have consciously asserted. Whereas the literal sense of Scripture describes a historical reality—a fact, precept, or event—the spiritual senses disclose deeper mysteries revealed through the historical realities. What the soul is to the body, the spiritual senses are to the literal. You can distinguish them; but if you try to separate them, death immediately follows. St. Paul was the first to insist upon this and warn of its consequences: "God . . . has qualified us to be ministers of a new covenant, not in a written code but in the Spirit; for the written code kills, but the Spirit gives life" (2 Cor 3:5–6).

Catholic tradition recognizes three spiritual senses that stand upon the foundation of the literal sense of Scripture (see CCC 115). (1) The first is the *allegorical* sense, which unveils the spiritual and prophetic meaning of biblical history. Allegorical interpretations thus reveal how persons, events, and institutions of Scripture can point beyond themselves toward greater mysteries yet to come (OT), or display the fruits of mysteries already revealed (NT). Christians have often read the Old Testament in this way to discover how the mystery of Christ in the New Covenant was once hidden in the Old, and how the full significance of the Old Covenant was finally made manifest in the New. Allegorical significance is likewise latent in the New Testament, especially in the life and deeds of Jesus recorded in the Gospels. Because Christ is the Head of the Church and the source of her spiritual life, what was accomplished in Christ the Head during his earthly life prefigures what he continually produces in his members through grace. The allegorical sense builds up the virtue of faith. (2) The second is the *tropological* or *moral* sense,

which reveals how the actions of God's people in the Old Testament and the life of Jesus in the New Testament prompt us to form virtuous habits in our own lives. It therefore draws from Scripture warnings against sin and vice, as well as inspirations to pursue holiness and purity. The moral sense is intended to build up the virtue of charity. (3) The third is the *anagogical* sense, which points upward to heavenly glory. It shows us how countless events in the Bible prefigure our final union with God in eternity, and how things that are "seen" on earth are figures of things "unseen" in heaven. Because the anagogical sense leads us to contemplate our destiny, it is meant to build up the virtue of hope. Together with the literal sense, then, these spiritual senses draw out the fullness of what God wants to give us through his Word and as such comprise what ancient tradition has called the "full sense" of Sacred Scripture.

All of this means that the deeds and events of the Bible are charged with meaning beyond what is immediately apparent to the reader. In essence, that meaning is Jesus Christ and the salvation he died to give us. This is especially true of the books of the New Testament, which proclaim Jesus explicitly; but it is also true of the Old Testament, which speaks of Jesus in more hidden and symbolic ways. The human authors of the Old Testament told us as much as they were able, but they could not clearly discern the shape of all future events standing at such a distance. It is the Bible's divine Author, the Holy Spirit, who could and did foretell the saving work of Christ, from the first page of the Book of Genesis onward.

The New Testament did not, therefore, abolish the Old. Rather, the New fulfilled the Old, and in doing so, it lifted the veil that kept hidden the face of the Lord's bride. Once the veil is removed, we suddenly see the world of the Old Covenant charged with grandeur. Water, fire, clouds, gardens, trees, hills, doves, lambs—all of these things are memorable details in the history and poetry of Israel. But now, seen in the light of Jesus Christ, they are much more. For the Christian with eyes to see, water symbolizes the saving power of Baptism; fire, the Holy Spirit; the spotless lamb, Christ crucified; Jerusalem, the city of heavenly glory.

The spiritual reading of Scripture is nothing new. Indeed the very first Christians read the Bible this way. St. Paul describes Adam as a "type" that prefigured Jesus Christ (Rom 5:14). A "type" is a real person, place, thing, or event in the Old Testament that foreshadows something greater in the New. From this term we get the word "typology", referring to the study of how the Old Testament prefigures Christ (CCC 128–30). Elsewhere St. Paul draws deeper meanings out of the story of Abraham's sons, declaring, "This is an allegory" (Gal 4:24). He is not suggesting that these events of the distant past never really happened; he is saying that the events both happened *and* signified something more glorious yet to come.

The New Testament later describes the Tabernacle of ancient Israel as "a copy and shadow of the heavenly sanctuary" (Heb 8:5) and the Mosaic Law as a "shadow of the good things to come" (Heb 10:1). St. Peter, in turn, notes that Noah and his family were "saved through water" in a way that "corresponds" to sacramental Baptism, which "now saves you" (1 Pet 3:20–21). Interestingly, the expression that is translated "corresponds" in this verse is a Greek term that denotes the fulfillment or counterpart of an ancient "type".

We need not look to the apostles, however, to justify a spiritual reading of the Bible. After all, Jesus himself read the Old Testament this way. He referred to Jonah (Mt 12:39), Solomon (Mt 12:42), the Temple (Jn 2:19), and the brazen serpent (Jn 3:14) as "signs" that pointed forward to him. We see in Luke's Gospel, as Christ comforted the disciples on the road to Emmaus, that "beginning with Moses and all the prophets, he interpreted to them in all the Scriptures the things concerning himself" (Lk 24:27). It was precisely this extensive spiritual interpretation of the Old Testament that made such an impact on these once-discouraged travelers, causing their hearts to "burn" within them (Lk 24:32).

Criteria for Biblical Interpretation. We too must learn to discern the "full sense" of Scripture as it includes both the literal and spiritual senses together. Still, this does not mean we should "read into" the Bible meanings that are not really there. Spiritual exegesis is not an unrestrained flight of the imagination. Rather, it is a sacred science that proceeds according to certain principles and stands accountable to sacred tradition, the Magisterium, and the wider community of biblical interpreters (both living and deceased).

In searching out the full sense of a text, we should always avoid the extreme tendency to "over-spiritualize" in a way that minimizes or denies the Bible's literal truth. St. Thomas Aquinas was well aware of this danger and asserted that "all other senses of Sacred Scripture are based on the literal" (*STh* I, 1, 10, *ad* 1, quoted in CCC 116). On the other hand, we should never confine the meaning of a text to the literal, intended sense of its human author, as if the divine Author did not intend the passage to be read in the light of Christ's coming.

Fortunately the Church has given us guidelines in our study of Scripture. The unique character and divine authorship of the Bible calls us to read it "in the Spirit" (*Dei Verbum* 12). Vatican II outlines this teaching in a practical way by directing us to read the Scriptures according to three specific criteria:

1. We must "[b]e especially attentive 'to the content and unity of the whole Scripture'" (CCC 112).

2. We must "[r]ead the Scripture within 'the living Tradition of the whole Church' " (CCC 113).

3. We must "[b]e attentive to the analogy of faith" (CCC 114; cf. Rom 12:6).

These criteria protect us from many of the dangers that ensnare readers of the Bible, from the newest inquirer to the most prestigious scholar. Reading Scripture out of context is one such pitfall, and probably the one most difficult to avoid. A memorable cartoon from the 1950s shows a young man poring over the pages of the Bible. He says to his sister: "Don't bother me now; I'm trying to find a Scripture verse to back up one of my preconceived notions." No doubt a biblical text pried from its context can be twisted to say something very different from what its author actually intended.

The Church's criteria guide us here by defining what constitutes the authentic "context" of a given biblical passage. The first criterion directs us to the literary context of every verse, including not only the words and paragraphs that surround it, but also the entire corpus of the biblical author's writings and, indeed, the span of the entire Bible. The *complete* literary context of any Scripture verse includes every text from Genesis to Revelation—because the Bible is a unified book, not just a library of different books. When the Church canonized the Book of Revelation, for example, she recognized it to be incomprehensible apart from the wider context of the entire Bible.

The second criterion places the Bible firmly within the context of a community that treasures a "living tradition". That community is the People of God down through the ages. Christians lived out their faith for well over a millennium before the printing press was invented. For centuries, few believers owned copies of the Gospels, and few people could read anyway. Yet they absorbed the gospel—through the sermons of their bishops and clergy, through prayer and meditation, through Christian art, through liturgical celebrations, and through oral tradition. These were expressions of the one "living tradition", a culture of living faith that stretches from ancient Israel to the contemporary Church. For the early Christians, the gospel could not be understood apart from that tradition. So it is with us. Reverence for the Church's tradition is what protects us from any sort of chronological or cultural provincialism, such as scholarly fads that arise and carry away a generation of interpreters before being dismissed by the next generation.

The third criterion places scriptural texts within the framework of faith. If we believe that the Scriptures are divinely inspired, we must also believe them to be internally coherent and consistent with all the doctrines that Christians believe. Remember, the Church's dogmas (such as the Real Presence, the papacy, the Immaculate Conception) are not

something *added* to Scripture, but are the Church's infallible interpretation *of* Scripture.

Using This Study Guide   This volume is designed to lead the reader through Scripture according to the Church's guidelines—faithful to the canon, to the tradition, and to the creeds. The Church's interpretive principles have thus shaped the component parts of this book, and they are designed to make the reader's study as effective and rewarding as possible.

Introductions: We have introduced the biblical book with an essay covering issues such as authorship, date of composition, purpose, and leading themes. This background information will assist readers to approach and understand the text on its own terms.

Annotations: The basic notes at the bottom of every page help the user to read the Scriptures with understanding. They by no means exhaust the meaning of the sacred text but provide background material to help the reader make sense of what he reads. Often these notes make explicit what the sacred writers assumed or held to be implicit. They also provide scores of historical, cultural, geographical, and theological information pertinent to the inspired narratives—information that can help the reader bridge the distance between the biblical world and his own.

Cross-References: Between the biblical text at the top of each page and the annotations at the bottom, numerous references are listed to point readers to other scriptural passages related to the one being studied. This follow-up is an essential part of any serious study. It is also an excellent way to discover how the content of Scripture "hangs together" in a providential unity. Along with biblical cross-references, the annotations refer to select paragraphs from the *Catechism of the Catholic Church*. These are not doctrinal "proof texts" but are designed to help the reader interpret the Bible in accordance with the mind of the Church. The *Catechism* references listed either handle the biblical text directly or treat a broader doctrinal theme that sheds significant light on that text.

Topical Essays, Word Studies, Charts: These features bring readers to a deeper understanding of select details. The *topical essays* take up major themes and explain them more thoroughly and theologically than the annotations, often relating them to the doctrines of the Church. Occasionally the annotations are supplemented by *word studies* that put readers in touch with the ancient languages of Scripture. These should help readers to understand better and appreciate the inspired terminology that runs throughout the sacred books. Also included are various *charts* that summarize biblical information "at a glance".

Icon Annotations: Three distinctive icons are

interspersed throughout the annotations, each one corresponding to one of the Church's three criteria for biblical interpretation. Bullets indicate the passage or passages to which these icons apply.

Notes marked by the book icon relate to the "content and unity" of Scripture, showing how particular passages of the Old Testament illuminate the mysteries of the New. Much of the information in these notes explains the original context of the citations and indicates how and why this has a direct bearing on Christ or the Church. Through these notes, the reader can develop a sensitivity to the beauty and unity of God's saving plan as it stretches across both Testaments.

Notes marked by the dove icon examine particular passages in light of the Church's "living tradition". Because the Holy Spirit both guides the Magisterium and inspires the spiritual senses of Scripture, these annotations supply information along both of these lines. On the one hand, they refer to the Church's doctrinal teaching as presented by various popes, creeds, and ecumenical councils; on the other, they draw from (and paraphrase) the spiritual interpretations of various Fathers, Doctors, and saints.

Notes marked by the key icon pertain to the "analogy of faith". Here we spell out how the mysteries of our faith "unlock" and explain one another. This type of comparison between Christian beliefs displays the coherence and unity of defined dogmas, which are the Church's infallible interpretations of Scripture.

Putting It All in Perspective   Perhaps the most important context of all we have saved for last: the interior life of the individual reader. What we get out of the Bible will largely depend on how we approach the Bible. Unless we are living a sustained and disciplined life of prayer, we will never have the reverence, the profound humility, or the grace we need to see the Scriptures for what they really are.

You are approaching the "word of God". But for thousands of years, since before he knit you in your mother's womb, the Word of God has been approaching you.

One Final Note. The volume you hold in your hands is only a small part of a much larger work still in production. Study helps similar to those printed in this booklet are being prepared for *all* the books of the Bible and will appear gradually as they are finished. Our ultimate goal is to publish a single, one-volume Study Bible that will include the entire text of Scripture, along with all the annotations, charts, cross-references, maps, and other features found in the following pages. Individual booklets will be published in the meantime, with the hope that God's people can begin to benefit from this labor before its full completion.

We have included a long list of Study Questions in the back to make this format as useful as possible, not only for individual study but for group settings and discussions as well. The questions are designed to help readers both "understand" the Bible and "apply" it to their lives. We pray that God will make use of our efforts and yours to help renew the face of the earth! «

INTRODUCTION TO THE GOSPEL ACCORDING TO JOHN

Author Unlike the Gospels according to Matthew, Mark, and Luke, the Gospel of John is not strictly anonymous. The author discreetly identifies himself as "the disciple whom Jesus loved" (21:20, 24) and claims to be an eyewitness to the life and ministry of Christ (1:14; 19:35). However, this Beloved Disciple never reveals his name, although he appears several times in the Gospel narrative (13:23; 19:26; 20:2).

The combined weight of textual and traditional evidence suggests that this disciple is the Apostle John, one of the sons of Zebedee (Mt 4:21). Several considerations support this conclusion. (1) The Beloved Disciple is clearly an Israelite, whose knowledge of biblical feasts and institutions is detailed and whose familiarity with Palestinian geography is quite accurate. (2) The Beloved Disciple is one of the Twelve who was present with Jesus at the Last Supper (13:23; Mk 14:17–25) and with the band of apostles after his Resurrection (21:4–7). (3) That he is "beloved" suggests he is part of the inner circle of disciples closest to Jesus: Peter, James, and John. These were the only apostles among the Twelve whom Jesus renamed in the written Gospel tradition (Mk 3:16–17) and the only apostles selected to accompany him at pivotal moments in his ministry (Mk 5:37; 9:2; 14:33). Since Peter is clearly distinguished from the Beloved Disciple (20:2; 21:20) and James was martyred far too early to be considered for authorship (Acts 12:2), John remains as the most likely candidate. (4) The close association between Peter and the Beloved Disciple in this Gospel (20:1–9) mirrors the close association between Peter and John in the writings of Luke (Lk 22:8; Acts 3:1; 8:14). (5) The attention to detail displayed by the author has all the earmarks of an eyewitness: he notices that the stone jars were filled "up to the brim" at Cana (2:7), the multiplied loaves were made of "barley" (6:9), and the aroma of the perfume used to anoint Jesus "filled" the house where the event took place (12:3). (6) As for external evidence, Irenaeus (A.D. 180), Clement of Alexandria (A.D. 200), and other early Christian writers testify with one voice that the Apostle John is the Beloved Disciple who wrote the Fourth Gospel, probably from the city of Ephesus in Asia Minor. Although John's authorship is disputed by many today, no alternative attempt to identify the Beloved Disciple aligns the evidence as clearly and convincingly as the traditional one.

Date Several scholars of the 19th and 20th centuries claimed the Gospel of John was written in the second century, some dating it as late as A.D. 150 and beyond. This is no longer tenable because of solid evidence to the contrary. For instance, a fragment of John's Gospel discovered in Egypt in 1935 has been dated as early as A.D. 120. The original Gospel must have been written at least by this time and probably much earlier, since ample time was needed for it to gain popularity and circulate from Asia Minor all the way to Africa. Likewise, Ignatius of Antioch seems to allude to the teaching of the Fourth Gospel in a collection of letters written about A.D. 107. This makes it probable that John's Gospel was composed at least before A.D. 100.

Whether it can be dated much earlier than this is a matter of dispute. Some have argued that John wrote his Gospel closer to the middle of the first century, even prior to the destruction of Jerusalem in A.D. 70. Interestingly, nothing within the Gospel demands a date later than this, and the casual statement in 5:2 that there "is" (present tense) a pool near the Sheep Gate in Jerusalem may lend support to its antiquity. It seems unlikely that John would have described this pool as though it were intact if, in fact, it was buried beneath a heap of rubble at the time he was writing about it. This makes a date in the 60s a viable option for the composition of John's Gospel, although most scholars prefer to date it in the 90s of the first century.

Destination and Purpose The Gospel of John was probably written for Jews and Jewish Christians living throughout the Mediterranean world. This is inferred from the distinctively Jewish flavor of the book and its numerous allusions to scriptural and liturgical symbols associated with Israel (1:1, 29, 45, 51; 2:21; 3:14; 4:10, etc.). Its positive depiction of the Samaritans, who were distant descendants of the Israelites, suggests they too were part of John's target audience (4:39–42). Although it was once popular to interpret John's Gospel against the backdrop of Greek culture and thought, more recent scholarship—especially since the discovery of the Dead Sea Scrolls—has led to a fuller appreciation of its Jewish background and themes.

Whatever the uncertainties of its destination, there is little uncertainty as to its aim. John tells us outright that his Gospel has an evangelistic purpose: "These are written that you may believe that Jesus is the Christ, the Son of God, and that believing you may have life in his name" (20:31). A secondary purpose, although unstated, seems to be to fill in some of the blanks left by Matthew, Mark,

and Luke. Whereas the Synoptic Gospels focus on Jesus' Galilean ministry and mention only one trip to Jerusalem, John tells us that Jesus made several trips to Jerusalem and mentions only brief excursions into the northern regions of Samaria and Galilee (1:43; 4:3–4; 11:54; 21:1). Whereas the Synoptics tell us of Jesus' ministry after the arrest of John the Baptist, the Fourth Gospel informs us that Jesus' ministry was already under way before John's imprisonment (3:24). Likewise, whereas the Synoptics narrate the Last Supper, John is silent about the eucharistic words and actions of Jesus, choosing instead to recount the Bread of Life discourse where Jesus first promises to give himself to the world as sacramental food (6:35–58). These differences have suggested to several scholars, ancient and modern alike, that John was familiar with one or more of the Synoptic Gospels. If so, he must have wanted to give readers additional information about the life and teaching of Jesus that would supplement the authentic Gospels already in circulation.

Themes and Characteristics The Fourth Gospel is a book of magnificent beauty and artistry. The richness of its expression and imagery has made it one of the most celebrated works in Christian history. So much of it is devoted to the heavenly identity and mission of Jesus that John was known as the "spiritual" Gospel in the ancient Church. Perhaps the most pervasive theme in John, which in many ways is the master key that unlocks the Gospel as a whole, is the revelation of God as a family. Nearly every chapter is marked by familial language that explains the inner life of God as well as our relation to God through the grace of divine generation.

The "divine family" of God revealed as Father, Son, and Spirit is the towering mystery of the Fourth Gospel. The Father initiates this revelation by sending his only Son, Jesus Christ, into the world as a man (1:14; 16:28). Through him we learn that the Father loves the Son (3:35), nourishes him with his will (4:34), and entrusts him with the responsibilities of judging and giving life to the world (5:22, 27). The divine unity between the Father and the Son is unlike any known on earth (10:30; 14:11). Christ, for his part, shows us the heart of his Father (1:18; 14:9) by imitating the Father's works (5:19–21; 10:25), speaking the Father's words (8:28; 12:49), and returning the Father's love (14:31). The essence of Jesus' divine Sonship is thus expressed through a lifetime of pleasing and honoring the Father (8:29, 49). The Spirit, too, is sent into the world by the Father and the Son (14:26; 15:26). His mission is to continue the ministry of Jesus, always teaching the truth (14:26), announcing things to come (16:13), and filling the hearts and lives of believers with his presence (14:17).

The "human family" also plays an important role in the Fourth Gospel. In fact, the heart of Jesus' message is that the children of men are invited to become children of God (1:12). This new life begins with a spiritual rebirth in Baptism (3:5) and is sustained as the Father nourishes us with divine food and drink (6:32, 51; 7:37–39), educates us in the truth (8:31–32; 16:13), and protects us from spiritual danger (17:15). Christ models the life of divine Sonship to perfection (13:15), showing us how to worship the Father (4:23–26), how to obey his commandments (15:10), and how to love our spiritual siblings (13:34). We are not left orphans (14:18) after Christ returns to the Father (20:17) because his presence dwells with us and even within us (14:17–18, 23). Our full union with the Trinity awaits only the coming of Jesus Christ, who will return in glory to escort the children of God into the house of their heavenly Father (14:2–3).

OUTLINE OF THE GOSPEL ACCORDING TO JOHN

1. Prologue (1:1–18)
    A. Christ, the Eternal Word (1:1–13)
    B. Christ, the Word Made Flesh (1:14–18)

2. The Book of Signs (1:19—12:50)
    A. The Witness of John and the Calling of Disciples (1:19–51)
    B. The Inaugural Signs of Jesus' Ministry (2:1—4:54)
    C. Healing on the Sabbath (5:1–47)
    D. The Bread of Life (6:1–71)
    E. The Feast of Tabernacles and the Sons of Abraham (7:1—8:59)
    F. The Light of the World (9:1–41)
    G. The Good Shepherd (10:1–42)
    H. The Raising of Lazarus (11:1–57)
    I. Triumphal Entry and the Rejection of Jesus (12:1–50)

3. The Book of Glory (13:1—20:31)
    A. The Foot Washing (13:1–30)
    B. The Last Supper Discourse (13:31—16:33)
    C. The High Priestly Prayer (17:1–26)
    D. The Passion Narrative (18:1—19:42)
    E. The Resurrection and Appearances (20:1–31)

4. Resurrection Epilogue (21:1–25)
    A. The Final Appearance and Miracle of Jesus (21:1–14)
    B. Jesus Questions and Commissions Peter (21:15–23)
    C. Conclusion (21:24–25)

THE GOSPEL ACCORDING TO

JOHN

The Word Became Flesh

1 In the beginning was the Word, and the Word was with God, and the Word was God. ²He was in the beginning with God; ³all things were made through him, and without him was not anything made that was made. ⁴In him was life,ᵃ and the life was the light of men. ⁵The light shines in the darkness, and the darkness has not overcome it.

6 There was a man sent from God, whose name was John. ⁷He came for testimony, to bear witness to the light, that all might believe through him. ⁸He was not the light, but came to bear witness to the light.

9 The true light that enlightens every man was coming into the world. ¹⁰He was in the world, and the world was made through him, yet the world knew him not. ¹¹He came to his own home, and his

---

1:1: Gen 1:1; 1 Jn 1:1; Rev 19:13; Jn 17:5.   **1:3:** Col 1:16; 1 Cor 8:6; Heb 1:2.   **1:4:** Jn 5:26; 11:25; 14:6.   **1:5:** Jn 9:5; 12:46.   **1:6:** Mk 1:4; Mt 3:1; Lk 3:2–3; Jn 1:19–23.   **1:9:** 1 Jn 2:8.

1:1–18 The Prologue functions like a musical overture, introducing the main themes of the Gospel to be developed in subsequent chapters: light (1:4), life (1:4), darkness (1:5), testimony (1:7), faith (1:12), glory (1:14), truth (1:17). This network of images and ideas is held together around Jesus the Word, who is portrayed as the Creator and Redeemer of all things. Similar poetic passages are found in Col 1:15–20 and Heb 1:1–4.

1:1 In the beginning: John traces the origin of the Word into eternity past, where God the Son was present with God the Father before time itself began (17:5). • This opening verse of John is a direct allusion to the opening verse of the Bible. As in Genesis 1, the evangelist draws attention to light, darkness, life, and the spoken Word that brought all things into existence (1:1–5). It is implied that the universe, once *created* through the Word of God, is now being *renewed* through that same Word come in the flesh as Jesus Christ (1:14; Rev 21:1–5; *Catechism of the Catholic Church* [hereafter CCC] 241, 291). **was with God:** Distinguishes the Word from the Father. They are not the same Person, yet they share the same nature in the family of the eternal Godhead (17:25–26) (CCC 254–56). **was God:** Or, "was divine". This is the first and clearest assertion of the deity of Jesus in the Fourth Gospel (5:18; 10:30–33; 20:28) (CCC 242).

1:4 life: Earthly life is a gift that is given and sustained by God through his eternal Word (Heb 1:3). Ultimately, natural and biological life points beyond itself to the supernatural and divine life that Jesus grants in abundance to the children of God (10:10; 2 Pet 1:4; CCC 1997). This new life comes to us when we give ourselves to Christ in faith (3:16; 20:31), and Christ gives himself to us through the sacramental action of the Church (3:5; 6:53).

1:5 light . . . darkness: Symbolic of the struggle between good and evil (1 Jn 2:8–11). Jesus himself is the true light (1:9) that drives away death, deception, and the devil (1 Jn 3:8). Other contrasts in the Gospel include flesh and Spirit (3:6), truth and falsehood (8:44–45), heaven and earth (3:31), and life and death (5:24).

1:6 John: John the Baptist, who fulfilled a divine mission to Israel (1:31) but was not the divine Messiah (1:20). Emphasis on John's subordinate role to Jesus runs throughout the Fourth Gospel, suggesting that one of the aims of the evangelist is to

win over the remaining band of John's disciples who had not yet accepted Jesus (3:25–30; 5:36; 10:41). Support for this is found in Acts 19:1–7, where we learn that a contingent of John's followers lived in Ephesus—the same city that tradition links with the publication of the Fourth Gospel. See introduction: *Author*.

1:10 the world: One of several concepts in John with multiple meanings. The world can refer (1) to the universe created by God (1:10), (2) to the fallen family of man in need of redemption (3:17), (3) and to the sphere of the devil that opposes God and hates the truth (15:18–20).

WORD STUDY

Word (1:1)

Logos (Gk.): "word", "statement", or "utterance". The term is used 330 times in the NT. The background of this concept in John is both philosophical and biblical. **(1)** Ancient Greek philosophers associated the Word with the order and design of the universe or with the intelligible expression of the mind of God as he sustains and governs it. **(2)** In biblical tradition the Word is the powerful utterance of God that brought all things into being at the dawn of time (Gen 1:3; Ps 33:6; Wis 9:1). **(3)** Another biblical tradition links the Word of God with the Wisdom of God, who was depicted as God's eternal companion (Prov 8:23; Sir 24:9), the craftsman who labored alongside God at creation (Prov 8:30; Wis 7:22), and the one who remains a source of life for the world (Prov 8:35). John, it seems, has pulled these traditions together to say something entirely new: the Word of God is not so much an abstract principle or an audible power as it is a Divine Person: God the Son (Rev 19:13). This eternal Word, once a mediator of creation, has now become a mediator of salvation through his Incarnation (1:14; 3:17).

ᵃ *Or was not anything made. That which has been made was life in him.*

own people received him not. [12]But to all who received him, who believed in his name, he gave power to become children of God; [13]who were born, not of blood nor of the will of the flesh nor of the will of man, but of God.

14 And the Word became flesh and dwelt among us, full of grace and truth; we have beheld his glory, glory as of the only-begotten Son from the Father. [15](John bore witness to him, and cried, "This was he of whom I said, 'He who comes after me ranks before me, for he was before me.'") [16]And from his fulness have we all received, grace upon grace. [17]For the law was given through Moses; grace and truth came through Jesus Christ. [18]No one has ever seen God; the only-begotten Son,[b] who is in the bosom of the Father, he has made him known.

The Testimony of John the Baptist

19 And this is the testimony of John, when the Jews sent priests and Levites from Jerusalem to ask him, "Who are you?" [20]He confessed, he did not deny, but confessed, "I am not the Christ." [21]And they asked him, "What then? Are you Eli´jah?" He said, "I am not." "Are you the prophet?" And he answered, "No." [22]They said to him then, "Who are you? Let us have an answer for those who sent us. What do you say about yourself?" [23]He said, "I am the voice of one crying in the wilderness, 'Make straight the way of the Lord,' as the prophet Isaiah said."

24 Now they had been sent from the Pharisees. [25]They asked him, "Then why are you baptizing, if you are neither the Christ, nor Eli´jah, nor the

---

1:12: Gal 3:26; Jn 3:18; 1 Jn 5:13.   **1:13:** Jn 3:5; 1 Pet 1:23; Jas 1:18; 1 Jn 3:9.
1:14: Rom 1:3; Gal 4:4; Phil 2:7; 1 Tim 3:16; Heb 2:14; 1 Jn 4:2.   **1:15:** Jn 1:30.   **1:16:** Col 1:19; 2:9; Eph 1:23; Rom 5:21.
1:17: Jn 7:19.   **1:18:** Ex 33:20; Jn 6:26; 1 Jn 4:12; Jn 3:11.   **1:19:** Jn 1:6.   **1:20:** Jn 3:28.
1:21: Mt 11:14; 16:14; Mk 9:13; Mt 17:13; Deut 18:15, 18.   **1:23:** Is 40:3; Mk 1:3; Mt 3:3; Lk 3:4.

1:11 received him not: Jesus' ministry to Israel was often resisted and sometimes rejected (8:56–59; 10:31; Lk 4:28–30).

1:12 believed in his name: i.e., believed that Jesus is the Messiah of Israel and the eternal Son of God (20:31; 1 Jn 5:1, 13). Names are inseparable from persons in Semitic thinking. So, for instance, the Lord himself is invoked when his name is called upon in worship (Gen 4:26; 12:8) and when covenants are ratified by swearing an oath in his name (Gen 21:23; 24:3). **children of God:** By the grace of divine generation we are filled with divine life and reborn as sons and daughters of the Father (1 Jn 3:1, 9). This transformation requires faith and takes place in Baptism (3:5–8; Gal 3:26–27) (CCC 2780–82).

📖 **1:13 not of blood . . . flesh . . . man:** Three means or processes that bring about natural birth into the world, i.e., women, the sexual impulse, and men. John is stressing that natural birth does not establish us in a supernatural relationship with God. • A similar cluster of ideas is found in Wis 7:1–2, where human existence is said to depend on the blood of prenatal gestation, the pleasure of marital relations, and the seed of man.

📖 **1:14 the Word became flesh:** Asserts the mystery of the Incarnation. It means that Christ, who is fully divine, eternal, and equal in being with the Father, came from heaven to earth and entered history as a man. The word "flesh" signifies all that is natural, earthly, and human (3:6; 6:63; 1 Jn 4:2) (CCC 423, 456–63). **dwelt among us:** The Greek means that Jesus "tabernacled" or "pitched his tent" among us (Rev 21:3). • John is making a link between the Incarnation of Jesus and the erection of the wilderness Tabernacle in the OT (Ex 25:8–9). The Tabernacle, once the architectural expression of Yahweh's presence in Israel, is a prophetic image of Jesus dwelling in our midst as a man. Likewise, as the Wisdom of God once tabernacled in Israel in the Torah of Moses (Sir 24:8), so Jesus is the embodiment of divine Wisdom in the flesh (1 Cor 1:24). See word study: *Word.* **grace and truth:** Equivalent to the "mercy and faithfulness" of God celebrated in the OT (Ex 34:6; Ps 25:10; 89:1; Prov 20:28; CCC 214). **his glory:** The magnificence of God's presence and Being once visible in the fiery cloud that indwelt the wilderness Tabernacle (Ex 40:34–35) and later the Jerusalem Temple (1 Kings 8:10–11). The glory of Christ is veiled behind his humanity and becomes visible only when he manifests it through his miracles (2:11; 11:40) (CCC 697).

1:15 ranks before me . . . was before me: The preeminence of Jesus over John is deduced from his preexistence. Although his ministry followed that of John, his life with the Father predated the foundations of the world itself (1:1; 8:58; 17:5).

1:16 grace upon grace: Or "grace in place of grace". As implied in the next verse, the graces of the Old Covenant have been superseded by the blessings of the New (1:17; CCC 504).

1:18 No one has ever seen God: God is pure spirit and thus invisible to human eyes (4:24; 1 Tim 6:16). Even still, the face of the Father can be seen in the face of Christ, who is the visible image of the invisible God (14:9; Col 1:15). Only in eternity will we see God as he truly is (1 Cor 13:12) (CCC 151). **the only-begotten Son:** A significant textual variant reads "God, the only begotten", which directly asserts the deity of Jesus. The reading followed in the translation can (1) refer to the eternal generation of Christ within the Trinity or (2) mean "unique" and "precious", as Isaac was the beloved of his father, Abraham (Heb 11:17) (CCC 444).

1:19 Jews: The term has a geographical tint and can sometimes be translated "Judeans". It has negative connotations in the Fourth Gospel because Jesus encounters great resistance in Judea (4:43–44) from the Judean leaders of Jerusalem who orchestrate his death (11:47–53; 19:12–16). The term is not a derogatory epithet directed at ethnic Jews in general; after all, Jesus was a Jew, as was his Mother, his disciples, and most of the earliest Christians (CCC 597). See note on 4:47.

1:20 the Christ: i.e., the Messiah (1:41). See word study: *Christ* at Mk 14.

📖 **1:21 Elijah?:** Israel anticipated the return of the prophet Elijah. • Malachi foretold that Elijah would make final preparations for the arrival of Israel's messianic Lord (Sir 48:10; Mal 4:5). John is not Elijah come again in the flesh, but he fulfills his mission in spirit (Lk 1:17) (CCC 718). See note on Mk 9:11. **the prophet?:** Israel awaited the coming of a prophet in the likeness of Moses. • That the authorities question whether John is *the* prophet and not simply a prophet suggests they are thinking of this Mosaic figure foretold in Deut 18:15–19. John is not the messianic prophet; it is Jesus who fulfills this role as the new Moses (4:20–26; 6:14; 7:40).

1:23 I am the voice: A quotation from Is 40:3. See note on Lk 3:4–6.

1:24 the Pharisees: The influential leaders of a Jewish renewal movement in NT Palestine. They are fierce opponents of Jesus and his message (7:45–53). See topical essay: *Who Are the Pharisees?* at Mk 2.

---

[b] Other ancient authorities read *God.*

prophet?" ²⁶John answered them, "I baptize with water; but among you stands one whom you do not know, ²⁷even he who comes after me, the thong of whose sandal I am not worthy to untie." ²⁸This took place in Bethany beyond the Jordan, where John was baptizing.

The Lamb of God

29 The next day he saw Jesus coming toward him, and said, "Behold, the Lamb of God, who takes away the sin of the world! ³⁰This is he of whom I said, 'After me comes a man who ranks before me, for he was before me.' ³¹I myself did not know him; but for this I came baptizing with water, that he might be revealed to Israel." ³²And John bore witness, "I saw the Spirit descend as a dove from heaven and remain on him. ³³I myself did not know him; but he who sent me to baptize with water said to me, 'He on whom you see the Spirit descend and remain, this is he who baptizes with the Holy Spirit.' ³⁴And I have seen and have borne witness that this is the Son of God."

The First Disciples of Jesus

35 The next day again John was standing with two of his disciples; ³⁶and he looked at Jesus as he walked, and said, "Behold, the Lamb of God!" ³⁷The two disciples heard him say this, and they followed Jesus. ³⁸Jesus turned, and saw them following, and said to them, "What do you seek?" And they said to him, "Rabbi" (which means Teacher), "where are you staying?" ³⁹He said to them, "Come and see." They came and saw where he was staying; and they stayed with him that day, for it was about the tenth hour. ⁴⁰One of the two who heard John speak, and followed him, was Andrew, Simon Peter's brother. ⁴¹He first found his brother Simon, and said to him, "We have found the Messiah" (which means Christ). ⁴²He brought him to Jesus. Jesus looked at him, and said, "So you are Simon the son of John? You shall be called Cephas" (which means Peter ᶜ).

Jesus Calls Philip and Nathanael

43 The next day Jesus decided to go to Galilee. And he found Philip and said to him, "Follow me." ⁴⁴Now Philip was from Beth-sa´ida, the city of Andrew and Peter. ⁴⁵Philip found Nathan´a-el, and said to him, "We have found him of whom Moses in the law and also the prophets wrote, Jesus of Nazareth, the son of Joseph." ⁴⁶Nathan´a-el said to

---

1:26–27: Mk 1:7–8; Mt 3:11; Lk3:16.　　**1:28:** Jn3:26; 10:40.　　**1:29:** Jn 1:36; Is 53:7; Acts 8:32; 1 Pet 1:19; Rev 5:6; 1 Jn 3:5.　　**1:30:** Jn 1:15.　　**1:32:** Mk 1:10; Mt 3:16; Lk 3:22.　　**1:35:** Lk 7:18.　　**1:40–42:** Mt 4:18–22; Mk 1:16–20; Lk 5:2–11.　　**1:41:** Dan 9:25; Jn 4:25.　　**1:42:** Jn 21:15–17; 1 Cor 15:5; Mt 16:18.

1:26 I baptize with water: The water baptism of John is merely a sign of the sacramental Baptism of Jesus. The former signified our need for cleansing and renewal; the latter effects this by an infusion of the grace and new life of the Spirit (Acts 2:38; Tit 3:5) (CCC 720, 1262).

1:28 Bethany: An unknown location east of the Jordan River (10:40). It is distinct from the Judean village of Bethany near Jerusalem (11:18).

1:29 Lamb of God: Points to the sacrificial dimension of Jesus' mission. ● This was *prefigured* by the Passover lambs of the Exodus, whose blood was a mark of divine protection for Israel and whose flesh was eaten in a liturgical meal (Ex 12:1–27), and *prophesied* by Isaiah, who portrayed the suffering Messiah as an innocent lamb slain for the sins of others (Is 53:7–12; CCC 608). See note on 12:32 and 19:36.

1:32 the Spirit descend as a dove: The Baptism of Jesus, which initiates his manifestation to Israel (1:31) and prefigures the effects of sacramental Baptism (3:1–13). See notes on Mt 3:15 and Mk 1:10. **remain:** The Greek expression is used often in John (also translated "dwell" or "abide") for the enduring bond between the Father and Son (14:10; 15:10) and for the indwelling of the Trinity in the believer (6:56; 14:17; 15:4–7).

1:35 two of his disciples: One of these is identified as "Andrew" (1:40), while the other is probably the evangelist himself. See introduction: *Author.*

1:39 the tenth hour: About 4 P.M. See note on Mt 20:1.

1:41 the Messiah: A rendering of the Hebrew word for "Anointed One". This title is rendered into Greek as **Christ** (4:25). See word study: *Christ* at Mk 14.

1:42 Cephas: A rendering of the Aramaic word *kepha'*, meaning "rock". With one exception from the fifth century B.C., this term was not generally used as a personal name before Jesus renamed Simon. The name **Peter** is its Greek equivalent. See word study: *Peter* at Mt 16.

1:44 Bethsaida: A village on the northern edge of the Sea of Galilee. **Nathanael:** Also called "Bartholomew" in the Synoptic Gospels. See chart: *The Twelve Apostles* at Mk 3.

1:45 Moses . . . the prophets: Introduces a theme of scriptural fulfillment that runs throughout the Gospel narrative (2:22; 5:46; 7:38; 10:35; etc.).

1:46 Nazareth: A secluded Galilean village considered unimportant to many in Israel.

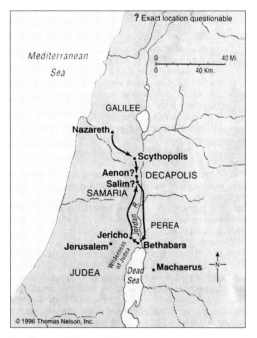

ᶜ From the word for *rock* in Aramaic and Greek, respectively.

Baptism and Temptation

him, "Can anything good come out of Nazareth?" Philip said to him, "Come and see." ⁴⁷Jesus saw Nathan´a-el coming to him, and said of him, "Behold, an Israelite indeed, in whom is no guile!" ⁴⁸Nathan´a-el said to him, "How do you know me?" Jesus answered him, "Before Philip called you, when you were under the fig tree, I saw you." ⁴⁹Nathan´a-el answered him, "Rabbi, you are the Son of God! You are the King of Israel!" ⁵⁰Jesus answered him, "Because I said to you, I saw you under the fig tree, do you believe? You shall see greater things than these." ⁵¹And he said to him, "Truly, truly, I say to you, you will see heaven opened, and the angels of God ascending and descending upon the Son of man."

The Marriage at Cana

2 On the third day there was a marriage at Cana in Galilee, and the mother of Jesus was there; ²Jesus also was invited to the marriage, with his disciples. ³When the wine failed, the mother of Jesus said to him, "They have no wine." ⁴And Jesus said to her, "O woman, what have you to do with me? My hour has not yet come." ⁵His mother said to the servants, "Do whatever he tells you." ⁶Now six stone jars were standing there, for the Jewish rites of purification, each holding twenty or thirty

---

1:43: Mt 10:3; Jn 6:5; 12:21; 14:8. **1:45:** Lk 24:27. **1:46:** Jn 7:41; Mk 6:2. **1:49:** Ps 2:7; Mk 15:32; Jn 12:13.
1:51: Lk 3:21; Gen 28:12. **2:1:** Jn 4:46; 21:2. **2:3:** Jn 19:26; Mk 3:31. **2:4:** Mk 1:24; 5:7; Jn 7:6, 30; 8:20.
2:6: Mk 7:3; Jn 3:25.

1:47 an Israelite indeed: i.e., a descendant of the patriarch Jacob, who was renamed "Israel" (Gen 32:28). Ironically, Jacob himself was known for his beguiling ways, especially when he intercepted the family blessing intended for his older brother Esau (Gen 27:35).

1:49 Son of God . . . King of Israel: Titles closely connected in ancient Israel, where King David and his successors are called the "sons" of Yahweh (2 Sam 7:14; Ps 2:7; 89:26–27). Unlike his Davidic predecessors, however, Jesus is the Son of God by nature and not by a covenant of divine adoption (1:18) (CCC 441–42). • Nathanael speaks from his knowledge of the OT. (1) That he was "called" while sitting "under the fig tree" (1:48) recalls how neighbors will "invite" one another under their "fig tree" in the messianic age (Zech 3:10). Judaism linked this hope with the coming of the royal "Branch", a messianic figure mentioned by Zechariah (Zech 3:8; 6:11–13) and modeled on his contemporary Zerubbabel, who rebuilt the Temple after the Exile (Hag 1:14; Zech 4:9). (2) Mention of Jesus' hometown suggests a connection with Is 11:1, where the "branch" that will sprout from David is a term (Heb. *netser*) linked to the word "Nazareth" (1:46). Once these oracles converged in the mind of Nathanael, he could reason that Jesus is the messianic "Branch" and thus the royal Son of God. • *Allegorically* (St. Augustine, *Tract. on John 7*, 21), the shade of the fig tree is the shadow of sin and death. Nathanael is the Church, who is known in advance by the mercy of God, cleansed of all guilt and impurity, and summoned by the apostles to come forth from darkness to live in the light.

1:51 ascending and descending: An allusion to Jacob's dream in Gen 28:11–15. • Jacob dreamed of a ladder spanning heaven and earth that enabled the angels to pass in and out of the world. Moved by the experience, he renamed the place where he slept "the house of God" and "the gate of heaven" (Gen 28:17). Jesus puts himself in the center of this vision, claiming that (1) he is the place where heaven touches down to earth; (2) he is the true house of God; and (3) he is the mediator through whom the angels exercise their ministry. See note on 2:19 and Heb 1:14. **the Son of man:** Alludes to the heavenly figure of Dan 7:13. See topical essay: *Jesus, the Son of Man* at Lk 17.

2:1 the third day: Chronologically, this refers to the third day since Jesus' encounter with Nathanael (1:43–51). Theologically, it has two levels of significance. (1) The third day is actually the seventh day of Jesus' opening week of ministry. The evangelist hints at this when he delineates the successive days in 1:29, 35, 43, and 2:1, implying that the creation fashioned in seven days (Gen 1:1–2:3) is being transformed and renewed through Jesus (2 Cor 5:17; Rev 21:1-5). (2) Jesus manifests his glory on the third day at Cana (2:11), just as he reveals his glory by rising on the third day after his death (1 Cor 15:4). See word study: *Signs*. **marriage at Cana:** Jewish weddings, like this one five miles north of Nazareth, could be celebrated for an entire week or more (Judg 14:12; Tob 11:19). Curiously, the young couple is never identified, leaving Jesus and his Mother to hold center stage for the entire episode (2:1–11). • Traditional exegesis holds that Jesus sanctifies the covenant of marriage by his presence at the wedding at Cana (CCC 1613).

2:3 the mother of Jesus: Mary is never called by her personal name in the Fourth Gospel (2:12; 19:25). **no wine:** An embarrassing predicament for the young couple. Mary's concern for the situation may suggest she is a relative of the wedding party. • Vatican II affirms the propriety of the title "Advocate" for the Mother of Jesus (*Lumen Gentium*, 62). It means that just as Mary intervened at Cana for the needs of others, so she continues to make heavenly intercession for the needs of the saints on earth (CCC 969).

2:4 woman: Although it might offend the standards of modern etiquette, this was a title of respect and endearment in antiquity (4:21; 8:10; 20:13). There is, however, no ancient example of a son addressing his mother in this way. • Genesis 3 is the reverse image of the Cana episode. As Eve prompted Adam to defy the Lord and drag the human family into sin, so Mary prompts Jesus, the new Adam, to initiate his mission of salvation. The description of Mary even alludes to Gen 3:15, where Yahweh speaks of a "woman" whose son will trample the devil underfoot (CCC 489, 494). **what have you to do with me?:** Or, what is that to you or to me?: A Hebrew idiom rendered in Greek. Its meaning is flexible and must be determined by context. In general, it can express either (1) disagreement between parties with divergent perspectives (1 Kings 17:18; 2 Kings 3:13; 2 Chron 35:21) or (2) the free consent of one party to the expressed will of another, with or without a sense of reluctance (Mk 1:24; 5:7; Lk 8:28). The second connotation fits this context since Jesus promptly complies with Mary's request (2:7-8) and Mary never wavers in her confidence that Jesus will respond favorably to her petition (2:5). **My hour has not yet come:** The assertion hides an important assumption. The statement would seem exaggerated unless the provision of wine was somehow connected with Jesus' appointed "hour". This points beyond the historical hour of his Passion to the commemoration of that hour in the eucharistic liturgy, where Christ is present behind the visible sign of wine (CCC 2618). See topical essay: *The "Hour" of Jesus* at Jn 4.

2:5 Do whatever he tells you: The final words of Mary in the NT, which ring out as her spiritual testament for all disciples of Jesus. • The command to follow Jesus echoes the command to follow Joseph in Gen 41:55. As the patriarch went on to provide bread in abundance during a time of famine, so Jesus supplies wine in abundance at a time of need.

2:6 six stone jars: Together holding over 120 gallons of water. • The purpose of these water jars is outlined in Num 19:11–22, which stipulates that any Israelite defiled by contact with the dead must be purified with water on the third

gallons. ⁷Jesus said to them, "Fill the jars with water." And they filled them up to the brim. ⁸He said to them, "Now draw some out, and take it to the steward of the feast." So they took it. ⁹When the steward of the feast tasted the water now become wine, and did not know where it came from (though the servants who had drawn the water knew), the steward of the feast called the bridegroom ¹⁰and said to him, "Every man serves the good wine first; and when men have drunk freely, then the poor wine; but you have kept the good wine until now." ¹¹This, the first of his signs, Jesus did at Cana in Galilee, and manifested his glory; and his disciples believed in him.

12 After this he went down to Caper′na-um, with his mother and his brethren and his disciples; and there they stayed for a few days.

The Cleansing of the Temple

13 The Passover of the Jews was at hand, and Jesus went up to Jerusalem. ¹⁴In the temple he found those who were selling oxen and sheep and pigeons, and the money-changers at their business. ¹⁵And making a whip of cords, he drove them all, with the sheep and oxen, out of the temple; and he poured out the coins of the money-changers and overturned their tables. ¹⁶And he told those who sold the pigeons, "Take these things away; you shall not make my Father's house a house of trade." ¹⁷His disciples remembered that it was written, "Zeal for your house will consume me." ¹⁸The Jews

---

2:11: Jn 2:23; 3:2; 4:54; 6:2.   **2:12:** Mt 4:13; Jn 7:3; Mk 3:31.   **2:13:** Jn 6:4; 11:55; Deut 16:1–6; Lk 2:41.
2:14–16: Mt 21:12–13; Mk 11:15–17; Lk 19:45–46.   **2:16:** Lk 2:49.   **2:17:** Ps 69:9.
2:18: Mk 11:28; Mt 21:23; Lk 20:2.

---

day and then again on the seventh day. Curiously, the Cana miracle takes place on the third day (2:1), which, according to John's chronology, is also the seventh day. See note on 2:1.
• The first sign performed by Jesus (water into wine) recalls the first sign performed by Moses (the first plague, water into blood, Ex 7:19). Note that wine is called the "blood" of the grape in Hebrew poetry (Gen 49:11; Deut 32:14).
2:9 the bridegroom: The unidentified groom at the wedding. Jesus fulfills this role on a spiritual level (3:29; Mt 25:1–13; CCC 796).
2:10 the good wine: A biblical symbol capable of many associations. (1) An abundance of wine is a sign of the messianic age (Is 25:6; Joel 3:18; Amos 9:13). (2) It signifies the joys of marital love (Song 1:2; 4:10; 7:9). (3) The transformation of water into wine anticipates the transubstantiation of wine into blood when Jesus gives himself to the world in the eucharistic liturgy (6:53; 1 Cor 10:16). (4) The wine of the marital celebra-

WORD STUDY

Signs (2:11)

Sēmeion (Gk.): a "sign" or "miracle". The term is used 17 times in John and 60 times in the rest of the NT. Since the signs in the Fourth Gospel are concentrated mainly in chaps. 1–12, the first half of John has been called the "Book of Signs". For the evangelist, the signs of Jesus are not just mighty works, but miracles that unveil the glory and power of God working through Christ. The signs of Jesus also recall the signs performed by Moses during the Exodus, signs that likewise revealed the glory of Yahweh (Num 14:22) working through Moses (Ex 3:12; 4:28–31; Deut 34:11). The Fourth Gospel draws attention to seven signs: **(1)** the miracle at Cana (2:1–11), **(2)** the healing of the official's son (4:46–54), **(3)** the healing of the paralytic (5:1–9), **(4)** the multiplication of the loaves (6:1–14), **(5)** the restoration of the blind man (9:1–41), **(6)** the raising of Lazarus (11:17–44), and, most important of all, **(7)** the Resurrection of Jesus, which is the second sign mentioned in the Gospel (2:18–22) but the final and climactic sign to be accomplished (20:1–10). Jesus elsewhere calls this the "sign of the prophet Jonah" (Mt 12:39).

tion looks beyond this life to the marriage supper of the Lamb in heaven (Rev 19:7–9) (CCC 1335).
2:12 Capernaum: A village on the northern shore of the Sea of Galilee and the headquarters of Jesus' Galilean ministry (Mt 4:13). **his brethren:** Not full brothers of Jesus but his close relatives (CCC 500). See note on Mt 12:46.
2:13 The Passover: Celebrated every spring to commemorate Israel's rescue from Egyptian slavery (Ex 12). Three times the Passover is mentioned in John, indicating that Jesus' ministry extended beyond two years (6:4; 13:1). See note on 6:4. **Jerusalem:** Nearly 80 percent of John's narrative places Jesus in Jerusalem. The Synoptic Gospels give greater attention to the ministry of Jesus in Galilee.
2:14–22 The cleansing of the Temple is recorded in all four Gospels. One difference among them is that John places the event at the *beginning* of Jesus' ministry, while the other Gospels place it at the *end* of his ministry. Two explanations for this are possible. (1) All four accounts may refer to the same event. If so, John moved the episode to the beginning of his narrative to highlight an important truth. As it stands, the Temple cleansing makes the same theological point as that in the preceding Cana episode: Jesus brings a New Covenant that supersedes the institutions of the Old. (2) Jesus may have cleansed the Temple twice. In fact, some have dated the episode in John around A.D. 27 or 28, calculating "forty-six years" from the time Herod the Great began renovating the Temple in 19 or 20 B.C. (2:20). This date fits more easily into the early period of Jesus' ministry than the latter part of it.
2:14 In the temple: The Jerusalem Temple was divided into several courts. The outermost court, open to Gentile pilgrims, was used for selling sacrificial animals and exchanging foreign currency for the appropriate coins needed to pay the annual Temple tax. Jesus is angry that the merchants are robbing Israel through inflated rates of exchange and robbing the Gentiles of the opportunity to worship and pray (CCC 583–84). See note on Mt 17:24.
2:15 poured out . . . overturned: The aggressive actions of Jesus are a prophetic sign of the Temple's imminent destruction (Mk 13:1–2). The expulsion of oxen, sheep, and pigeons (2:14) from the precincts likewise signifies the termination of animal sacrifice in the Temple (4:21–24). See note on Mk 11:15. • Allegorically (Origen, *Comm. in Jo.* 10, 16), the sanctuary is the undisciplined soul, filled, not with animals and merchants, but with earthly and senseless attachments. Christ must expel them with the whip of his divine doctrine to make spiritual worship possible.
2:17 Zeal for your house: A reference to Ps 69:9. • Psalm 69 depicts the suffering of the righteous, who are pained by the insults that sinners heap upon God. Jesus, burning with

then said to him, "What sign have you to show us for doing this?" [19]Jesus answered them, "Destroy this temple, and in three days I will raise it up." [20]The Jews then said, "It has taken forty-six years to build this temple, and will you raise it up in three days?" [21]But he spoke of the temple of his body. [22]When therefore he was raised from the dead, his disciples remembered that he had said this; and they believed the Scripture and the word which Jesus had spoken.

23 Now when he was in Jerusalem at the Passover feast, many believed in his name when they saw the signs which he did; [24]but Jesus did not trust himself to them, [25]because he knew all men and needed no one to bear witness of man; for he himself knew what was in man.

Nicodemus Visits Jesus

3 Now there was a man of the Pharisees, named Nicode´mus, a ruler of the Jews. [2]This man came to Jesus [d] by night and said to him, "Rabbi, we know that you are a teacher come from God; for no one can do these signs that you do, unless God is with him." [3]Jesus answered him, "Truly, truly, I say to you, unless one is born anew,[e] he cannot see the kingdom of God." [4]Nicode´mus said to him, "How can a man be born when he is old? Can he enter a second time into his mother's womb and be born?" [5]Jesus answered, "Truly, truly, I say to you, unless one is born of water and the Spirit, he cannot enter the kingdom of God. [6]That which is born of the flesh is flesh, and that which is born of the Spirit is spirit.[f] [7]Do not marvel that I said to you, 'You must be born anew.'[e] [8]The wind[f] blows where it wills, and you hear the sound of it, but you do not know where it comes from or where it goes; so it is with every one who is born of the Spirit." [9]Nicode´mus said to him, "How can this be?" [10]Jesus answered him, "Are you a teacher of Israel, and yet you do not understand this? [11]Truly, truly, I say to you, we speak of what we know, and bear witness to what we have seen; but you do not receive our testimony. [12]If I have told you earthly things and you do not believe, how can you believe if I tell you heavenly things? [13]No one has ascended into heaven but he who descended from heaven, the Son of man.[g] [14]And as Moses lifted up the serpent in the wilderness, so must the Son of man be lifted up, [15]that whoever believes in him may have eternal life."[h]

2:19: Mk 14:58; Acts 6:14.   2:21: 1 Cor 6:19; Jn 8:57.   2:22: Jn 12:16; 14:26.   2:25: Jn 1:47; 6:61; 13:11; Mk 2:8.
3:1: Jn 7:50; 19:39; Lk 23:13; Jn 7:26.   3:2: Jn 2:11; 7:31; 9:16; Acts 10:38.   3:3: Jn 1:13; 1 Pet 1:23; Jas 1:18; 1 Jn 3:9.
3:5: Ezek 36:25–27; Eph 5:26; Tit 3:5.   3:6: 1 Cor 15:50.   3:8: Ezek 37:9.   3:11: Jn 8:26; 1:18; 3:32.
3:13: Rom 10:6; Eph 4:9.   3:14: Num 21:9; Jn 8:28; 12:34.

---

righteous indignation, is outraged that business dealings have taken the place of prayer in the Temple courts.

2:19 Destroy this temple: Jesus challenges his critics to destroy, not the sacred building, but his own body (2:21–22). Ironically, the latter is destined to replace the former: after the Crucifixion, the Temple of Jerusalem will be razed to the ground in divine judgment while the temple of Jesus' body will be raised from the grave in divine glory (CCC 586, 994).

2:25 he knew all men: The supernatural knowledge of Jesus is often highlighted in the Gospels (4:39; 16:30; Mt 9:4; 17:27; Mk 11:2–4; Lk 22:9–13). Here he detects deficient faith in those who marvel at his miracles but fail to grasp the significance of his mission. In the next episode, Nicodemus is representative of such inadequate belief (3:1–15) (CCC 473).

3:1 Nicodemus: Probably a member of the Jewish court, the Sanhedrin. See note on Mk 14:55.

3:2 by night: Nicodemus comes to Jesus under the cover of darkness because he fears persecution from the unbelieving leaders of Israel (12:42; 19:38). Symbolically, he is walking in spiritual darkness and lacks the enlightenment of true faith (8:12).

3:3 anew: The Greek expression can mean either "again" or "from above". Nicodemus takes it to mean "again", as though Jesus required a physical rebirth to enter his kingdom. This is a misunderstanding. Jesus instead calls for a spiritual rebirth "from above" (CCC 526). The Greek expression always means "from above" elsewhere in John (3:31; 19:11, 23).

3:5 born of water and the Spirit: The syntax of this verse in Greek suggests that Jesus is speaking, not of two separate births, one by water and another by the Spirit, but of a single birth through the working of water and Spirit together. Several observations suggest the verse refers to the Sacrament of Baptism. (1) A close link between water and Spirit is forged elsewhere in John's writings (7:38–39; 1 Jn 5:8). This

is most explicit in 1:33, where the Spirit descends upon Jesus at the very moment he is baptized in the waters of the Jordan. (2) Immediately following this episode Jesus and the disciples begin a baptismal ministry in Judea (3:22). (3) Other NT passages describe Baptism as a sacrament of salvation through the Spirit (Acts 2:38; 1 Cor 6:11; Tit 3:5; 1 Pet 3:21). ● The OT envisions Yahweh pouring out his Spirit from above in the messianic age (Is 32:15; Ezek 39:29; Joel 2:28–29). This was depicted as water being poured upon the Israelites to wash away their iniquities and renew their hearts (Is 44:3; Ezek 36:25–26). These prophetic hopes should have prepared Nicodemus to understand the thrust of Jesus' teaching (3:10). ● The Council of Trent declared in 1547 that Jn 3:5 refers to Baptism. It was said that "water" is no mere metaphor, but a visible sign of the Spirit's invisible work in the sacrament (Sess. 7, can. 2) (CCC 694, 1215, 1257).

3:6 flesh . . . spirit: A significant contrast in John. Flesh represents all that is natural, earthly, and human, while spirit signifies all that is supernatural, heavenly, and divine. The distance once separating these realms has been bridged by Jesus Christ, whose flesh (1:14) is an instrument that conveys the life and Spirit of God to the world (5:21; 6:51–53; 20:22).

3:8 The wind blows: Or "The Spirit blows" (see textual note f). By capitalizing on the double meaning of this expression, Jesus reasons that if the direction and destiny of the wind is mysterious, then the mission of the Holy Spirit is even more so in the lives of believers (CCC 691).

3:11 our testimony: i.e., the twofold witness of Jesus and John the Baptist (1:7, 19; 3:28).

3:14 the serpent: A reference to the episode in Num 21:4–9. ● Moses hoisted a bronze serpent upon a pole as a remedy for faithless Israel. Although God punished them with poisonous serpents, he promised to save everyone who looked to the bronze serpent in search of his mercy. Jesus sees this relic as an image of his own Crucifixion and the healing it will bring to a rebellious world (CCC 2130). **be lifted up:** A shorthand reference to the Paschal Mystery, when Jesus is lifted up *on* the Cross, *from* the grave, and *into* heaven (8:28; 12:32).

---

[d] Greek *him*.   [e] Or *from above*.
[f] The same Greek word means both *wind* and *spirit*.
[g] Other ancient authorities add *who is in heaven*.
[h] Some interpreters hold that the quotation continues through verse 21.

16 For God so loved the world that he gave his only-begotten Son, that whoever believes in him should not perish but have eternal life. ¹⁷For God sent the Son into the world, not to condemn the world, but that the world might be saved through him. ¹⁸He who believes in him is not condemned; he who does not believe is condemned already, because he has not believed in the name of the only-begotten Son of God. ¹⁹And this is the judgment, that the light has come into the world, and men loved darkness rather than light, because their deeds were evil. ²⁰For every one who does evil hates the light, and does not come to the light, lest his deeds should be exposed. ²¹But he who does what is true comes to the light, that it may be clearly seen that his deeds have been wrought in God.

Jesus and John the Baptist

22 After this Jesus and his disciples went into the land of Judea; there he remained with them and baptized. ²³John also was baptizing at Ae´non near Salim, because there was much water there; and people came and were baptized. ²⁴For John had not yet been put in prison.

25 Now a discussion arose between John's dis-

ciples and a Jew over purifying. ²⁶And they came to John, and said to him, "Rabbi, he who was with you beyond the Jordan, to whom you bore witness, here he is, baptizing, and all are going to him." ²⁷John answered, "No one can receive anything except what is given him from heaven. ²⁸You yourselves bear me witness, that I said, I am not the Christ, but I have been sent before him. ²⁹He who has the bride is the bridegroom; the friend of the bridegroom, who stands and hears him, rejoices greatly at the bridegroom's voice; therefore this joy of mine is now full. ³⁰He must increase, but I must decrease." *ⁱ*

He Who Comes from Heaven

31 He who comes from above is above all; he who is of the earth belongs to the earth, and of the earth he speaks; he who comes from heaven is above all. ³²He bears witness to what he has seen and heard, yet no one receives his testimony; ³³he who receives his testimony sets his seal to this, that God is true. ³⁴For he whom God has sent utters the words of God, for it is not by measure that he gives the Spirit; ³⁵the Father loves the Son, and has given all things into his hand.

3:16: Rom 5:8; 8:32; Eph 2:4; 1 Jn 4:9–10.   **3:17:** Jn 8:15; 12:47; Lk 19:10; 1 Jn 4:14.   **3:19:** Jn 1:4; 8:12; Eph 5:11, 13.
3:21: 1 Jn 1:6.   **3:22:** Jn 4:2.   **3:24:** Mk 1:14; 6:17–18.   **3:26:** Jn 1:7, 28.   **3:27:** 1 Cor 4:7.   **3:28:** Jn 1:20, 23.
3:29: Mk 2:19–20; Mt 25:1; Jn 15:11.   **3:31:** Jn 3:13; 8:23; 1 Jn 4:5.   **3:32:** Jn 3:11.

3:16 gave his only-begotten Son: The earthly mission of Jesus is part of the heavenly plan of the Father, who displays the depth of his love through the sacrifice of his Son (Rom 5:8; 1 Jn 3:16; CCC 219). This verse marks a transition from the dialogue between Jesus and Nicodemus (3:1–15) to an extended monologue by either Jesus or the evangelist himself (3:16–21). **eternal life:** The expression refers both to the *divine* quality of new life in Christ as well as its *duration*. We receive this gift already on earth in the hope that we will possess it irrevocably in heaven (10:10; 1 Jn 5:13).
3:18 condemned already: Unbelief is a form of rebellion that puts offenders outside the safety of the covenant. To reject the Son of God is to reject the light of faith in preference to spiritual darkness, death, and disinheritance (3:20; CCC 679).
3:22 baptized: Clarification is made in 4:2 that only the disciples of Jesus were baptizing.
3:23 Aenon: An uncertain location, probably in either Samaria (central Palestine) or the Jordan Valley (eastern Palestine).
3:24 put in prison: John is imprisoned for reprimanding Herod Antipas, ruler of Galilee. See note on Mk 6:18.
3:25–30 The ministry of John the Baptist is of real but secondary importance compared to the saving mission of Jesus. John humbly recognizes this and so directs his disciples to become followers of Christ. See note on 1:6.
3:29 the bridegroom: Jesus, whose bride is the Church (2 Cor 11:2; Eph 5:21–32). John the Baptist is the friend or "best man" of the groom who, in Jewish custom, arranges and manages the wedding celebration. John is content to fade into the background now that his duties are fulfilled (3:30).
• The marital covenant between Jesus and the Church is an extension of the spousal relation between Yahweh and Israel under the Old Covenant (Is 54:5–8; Jer 2:2; Hos 2:16–20; CCC 796; 1612).
3:31 earth . . . heaven: A contrast between the earthly ori-

gin and ministry of John the Baptist and the heavenly origin and ministry of Jesus Christ.
3:34 not by measure: As the Messiah, Jesus possesses the fullness of the Spirit (Is 11:2) and his graces (1:16) (CCC 504).

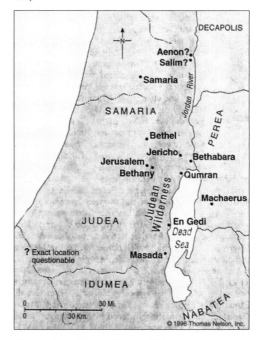

The Region of John the Baptist

ⁱ Some interpreters hold that the quotation continues through verse 36.

³⁶He who believes in the Son has eternal life; he who does not obey the Son shall not see life, but the wrath of God rests upon him.

Jesus and the Woman of Samaria

4 Now when the Lord knew that the Pharisees had heard that Jesus was making and baptizing more disciples than John ²(although Jesus himself did not baptize, but only his disciples), ³he left Judea and departed again to Galilee. ⁴He had to pass through Samar´ia. ⁵So he came to a city of Samar´ia, called Sy´char, near the field that Jacob gave to his son Joseph. ⁶Jacob's well was there, and so Jesus, wearied as he was with his journey, sat down beside the well. It was about the sixth hour.

7 There came a woman of Samar´ia to draw water. Jesus said to her, "Give me a drink." ⁸For his disciples had gone away into the city to buy food. ⁹The Samaritan woman said to him, "How is it that you, a Jew, ask a drink of me, a woman of Samar´ia?" For Jews have no dealings with Samaritans. ¹⁰Jesus answered her, "If you knew the gift of God, and who it is that is saying to you, 'Give me a drink,' you would have asked him and he would have given you living water." ¹¹The woman said to him, "Sir, you have nothing to draw with, and the well is deep; where do you get that living water? ¹²Are you greater than our father Jacob, who gave us the well, and drank from it himself, and his sons, and his cattle?" ¹³Jesus said to her, "Every one who drinks of this water will thirst again, ¹⁴but whoever drinks of the water that I shall give him will never thirst; the water that I shall give him will become in him a spring of water welling up to eternal life." ¹⁵The woman said to him, "Sir, give me this water, that I may not thirst, nor come here to draw."

16 Jesus said to her, "Go, call your husband, and come here." ¹⁷The woman answered him, "I have no husband." Jesus said to her, "You are right in saying, 'I have no husband'; ¹⁸for you have had five husbands, and he whom you now have is not your husband; this you said truly." ¹⁹The woman said to him, "Sir, I perceive that you are a prophet. ²⁰Our fathers worshiped on this mountain; and you say that in Jerusalem is the place to worship." ²¹Jesus said to her, "Woman, believe me, the hour is coming when neither on this mountain nor in Jerusalem will you worship the Father. ²²You worship what you do not know; we worship what we know, for salvation is from the Jews.

3:36: Jn 3:16; 5:24.   **4:1:** Jn 3:22.   **4:4:** Lk 9:52; 17:11.   **4:5:** Gen 33:19; 48:22; Josh 24:32.   **4:9:** Mt 10:5; Jn 8:48; Ezra 4:3–6.   **4:10:** Jn 7:37; Rev 21:6; 22:17.   **4:14:** Jn 6:35; 7:38.   **4:15:** Jn 6:34.   **4:18:** 2 Kings 17:24; Hos 2:7.   **4:20:** Deut 11:29; Josh 8:33; Lk 9:53.   **4:21:** Jn 5:25; 16:2, 32; Mal 1:11.   **4:22:** 2 Kings 17:28–41; Is 2:3; Rom 9:4.

3:36 believes . . . does not obey: Faith is exercised when we trust in God and entrust ourselves to God. Because it involves both the *assent* of the mind and the *consent* of the will, it can never be a purely intellectual decision that exists independently of one's behavior (Jas 2:14–26). It is because faith and faithfulness are two sides of the same coin that the opposite of faith is not just unbelief, but disobedience (CCC 161).

4:4 had to pass through: A divine necessity, dictated not by geography but by the missionary schedule given to Jesus by the Father. Jews normally traveled a longer route from Judea to Galilee by skirting around the eastern side of Samaria along the Jordan River.

4:5 Sychar: Probably ancient Shechem, where Jacob purchased a field (Gen 33:18–20).

4:6 Jacob's well: Nowhere mentioned in the OT but traditionally located at the foot of Mt. Gerizim in central Samaria. • The setting recalls the marital arrangements described in the Pentateuch. As the wives of Isaac (Gen 24:10–67), Jacob (Gen 29:1–30), and Moses (Ex 2:15–21) were first encountered at a well, so Jesus is the divine bridegroom in search of believers to be his covenant bride (3:29). **the sixth hour:** About noon.

4:7–42 Centuries of animosity between Jews and Samaritans loom in the background of this episode. It began with the devastation of northern Palestine by Assyria in the eighth century B.C., when masses of Israelites were deported out of the land and foreign peoples were forcibly resettled in the region (2 Kings 17:6, 24–41). According to the Jews of southern Palestine, the remaining Israelites (Samaritans) had defiled themselves by assimilating the practices of these pagan peoples and intermarrying with them. The enmity between Jews and Samaritans was very much alive in NT times, and both groups took steps to avoid interaction with one another, especially in matters of food and drink.

4:9 How is it . . . ? Jesus oversteps the boundaries of Jewish tradition, which discouraged men from conversing with women in public (4:27), sharing a drink with a Samaritan (4:7), or associating with a recognized sinner (4:18).

4:10 living water: An expression with two levels of meaning. The woman takes it to mean "flowing" water, i.e., a preferable alternative to stagnant well water (4:11–12). Jesus, however, is speaking of the life and vitality of the Spirit (7:38–39; CCC 728, 2560). • Several prophetic texts depict the blessings of the Lord as life-giving "water" (Is 12:3; 44:3; Ezek 47:1–12; Zech 14:8). See note on 3:5. • Christian tradition associates living water with baptismal waters, which lead us to "eternal life" (4:14). Paul, in fact, describes Baptism in terms of drinking from the Spirit (1 Cor 12:13; CCC 694).

4:15 Sir: A respectful term of address. As the episode progresses, the perception of Jesus' identity becomes ever more clear: by 4:19 he is a "prophet", by 4:29 he is the "Christ", and by 4:42 he is the "Savior of the world".

4:18 five husbands: The woman has endured multiple marital struggles. • The woman's personal life parallels the historical experience of the Samaritan people. According to 2 Kings 17:24–31, the five foreign tribes who intermarried with the northern Israelites (Samaritans) introduced five male deities into their religion. These idols were individually addressed as *Baal*, a Hebrew word meaning "lord" or "husband". The prophets denounced Israel for serving these gods, calling such worship infidelity to its true covenant spouse, Yahweh. Hope was kept alive, however, that God would show mercy to these Israelites and become their everlasting husband in the bonds of a New Covenant (Hos 2:16–20). This day has dawned in the ministry of Jesus, the divine bridegroom (3:29), who has come to save the Samaritans from a lifetime of struggles with five pagan "husbands". See note on 4:6.

4:20 on this mountain: In OT times the Samaritans worshiped in a sanctuary built on Mt. Gerizim. Although it was destroyed in 128 B.C., they continued to worship on the mountain during NT times and even to the present day.

4:22 what you do not know: Samaritan religion was an admixture of Israelite faith and pagan idolatry (2 Kings 17:29–34). • Jesus speaks from the perspective of the OT, which describes idol worship as ignorant worship (Wis 13:1–2, 10–19; Is 44:9–20). **from the Jews:** The Messiah was expected

²³But the hour is coming, and now is, when the true worshipers will worship the Father in spirit and truth, for such the Father seeks to worship him. ²⁴God is spirit, and those who worship him must worship in spirit and truth." ²⁵The woman said to him, "I know that Messiah is coming (he who is called Christ); when he comes, he will show us all things." ²⁶Jesus said to her, "I who speak to you am he."

27 Just then his disciples came. They marveled that he was talking with a woman, but none said, "What do you wish?" or, "Why are you talking with her?" ²⁸So the woman left her water jar, and went away into the city, and said to the people, ²⁹"Come, see a man who told me all that I ever did. Can this be the Christ?" ³⁰They went out of the city and were coming to him.

31 Meanwhile the disciples begged him, saying, "Rabbi, eat." ³²But he said to them, "I have food to eat of which you do not know." ³³So the disciples said to one another, "Has any one brought him food?" ³⁴Jesus said to them, "My food is to do the will of him who sent me, and to accomplish his work. ³⁵Do you not say, 'There are yet four months, then comes the harvest'? I tell you, lift up your eyes, and see how the fields are already white for harvest. ³⁶He who reaps receives wages, and gathers fruit for eternal life, so that sower and reaper may rejoice together. ³⁷For here the saying holds true, 'One sows and another reaps.' ³⁸I sent you to reap that for which you did not labor; others have labored, and you have entered into their labor."

39 Many Samaritans from that city believed in him because of the woman's testimony, "He told me all that I ever did." ⁴⁰So when the Samaritans came to him, they asked him to stay with them; and he stayed there two days. ⁴¹And many more believed because of his word. ⁴²They said to the woman, "It is no longer because of your words that we believe, for we have heard for ourselves, and we know that this is indeed the Savior of the world."

Jesus Departs for Galilee

43 After the two days he departed to Galilee. ⁴⁴For Jesus himself testified that a prophet has no honor in his own country. ⁴⁵So when he came to Galilee, the Galileans welcomed him, having seen all that he had done in Jerusalem at the feast, for they too had gone to the feast.

Jesus Heals an Official's Son

46 So he came again to Cana in Galilee, where he had made the water wine. And at Caper´na-um there was an official whose son was ill. ⁴⁷When he heard that Jesus had come from Judea to Galilee, he went and begged him to come down and heal his son, for he was at the point of death. ⁴⁸Jesus therefore said to him, "Unless you see signs and wonders you will not believe." ⁴⁹The official said to him, "Sir, come down before my child dies." ⁵⁰Jesus said to him, "Go; your son will live." The man believed the word that Jesus spoke to him and went his way. ⁵¹As he was going down, his servants met him and told him that his son was living. ⁵²So he asked them the hour when he began to mend, and they said to him, "Yesterday at the seventh hour the fever left

---

4:24: Phil 3:3.   **4:26:** Jn 8:24.   **4:29:** Jn 7:26; Mt 12:23.   **4:32:** Mt 4:4.   **4:34:** Jn 5:30; 6:38; 17:4.
4:35: Lk 10:2; Mt 9:37.   **4:37:** Job 31:8; Mic 6:15.   **4:42:** 1 Jn 4:14; 2 Tim 1:10.   **4:44:** Mk 6:4; Mt 13:57.
4:46: Jn 2:1–11; Mt 8:5–10; Lk 7:2–10.   **4:48:** Dan 4:2; Mk 13:22; Acts 2:19; 4:30; Rom 15:19; Heb 2:4.

---

to come from the line of King David, who belonged to the royal tribe of Judah (Gen 49:8–12).

4:23 in spirit and truth: Christian worship contrasts with Jewish and Samaritan worship. It will be in *spirit*, not confined to a single Israelite sanctuary where the ritual sacrifice of animals has continued since the days of Moses. It will also be in *truth*, not tainted by the errors of idolatry that have plagued the Samaritans since the days of the divided kingdom. See topical essay: The *"Hour"* of Jesus (page 26)

4:26 I . . . am he: Jesus accepts the title "Messiah" (4:25) only here and at his trial (Mk 14:61–62). See note on Mk 1:44.

🕊 **4:28 left her water jar:** The woman becomes both a believer and a missionary, accepting Jesus as the Messiah and sharing that belief with her hometown (4:39–42). • *Morally* (St. Augustine, *Tract. on John* 15, 16, 30), the water jar is the fallen desire of man that draws pleasure from the dark wells of the world but is never satisfied for long. Conversion to Christ moves us, like the Samaritan woman, to renounce the world, leave behind the desires of our earthen vessels, and follow a new way of life.

4:34 My food: The Father's will will always be the driving force behind Jesus' mission (5:19; 6:38; 12:49; 14:10; etc.).

4:35 white for harvest: Suggests that the world in general and the Samaritans in particular are ripe and ready to be gathered by the missionary efforts of the Church (Acts 8:4–25; Rev 14:14–16).

4:42 the Savior: A title for Jesus also in Lk 2:11 and 1 Jn 4:14. Although salvation comes *from* the Jews (4:22), it is *for* all the nations of the world (3:17; 1 Jn 2:2).

4:44 a prophet has no honor: A similar proverb is uttered when Jesus is rejected by his hometown of Nazareth (Lk 4:24). The remark resonates with bitter irony: although Jesus is a Jew (4:9), he is rejected by kinsmen from his own country of Judea (4:3, 47). See note on 1:19.

4:46 Capernaum: This village was more than 15 miles from Cana. The official from the town was probably a royal officer under Herod Antipas, ruler of Galilee. A similar episode where Jesus heals from a distance appears in Mt 8:5–13 and Lk 7:1–10.

4:47 Judea to Galilee: Geography plays a symbolic role in John. For the most part, the northern regions of Samaria and Galilee accept Jesus in faith (1:43–49; 2:11; 4:39, 53–54), whereas the southern region of Judea with its capital in Jerusalem is persistently antagonistic toward him (5:18; 7:1; 9:22; 10:33; 11:7–8, etc.). This tension between north and south is underscored by repeated emphasis on Jesus' withdrawal from Judea to Galilee (4:3, 45, 46, 54) and elsewhere when the Judean opponents of Jesus make derogatory remarks about Galileans and Samaritans (7:52; 8:48). It is against this background that John classifies the enemies of Christ as "the Jews", i.e., the unbelieving leaders of Judea and Jerusalem. See note on 1:19.

4:52 the seventh hour: About 1 P.M. See note on Mt 20:1.

The "Hour" of Jesus

SEVENTEEN times the Gospel of John mentions of the "hour" of Jesus. In the first half of the book, the "hour" is a highly anticipated moment in the ministry of Jesus that constantly grabs the attention of the reader and drives the narrative forward (2:4; 4:21; 5:25; 7:30, 8:20). In the second half of the book, readers discover that Jesus comes upon his "hour" only in the final days of his life (12:23, 27; 13:1; 17:1). What is the meaning of this "hour", and why was it the singular focus of Jesus' mission?

A careful analysis of the Fourth Gospel reveals two dimensions of this mysterious "hour", one rooted in the historical life of Christ and another in the liturgical life of the Church.

THE HISTORICAL HOUR

The "hour" of Christ is first and foremost the appointed time of his Passion, which in John, as in all the Gospels, is the climactic phase of his mission. Before this time the attempts of Jesus' enemies to arrest him are in vain because his "hour" has not yet come (7:30; 8:20). The clock begins ticking, however, at the start of Passion Week, when Jesus declares that the "hour" of his glorification has at last arrived (12:23). Although troubled by the painful ordeal that will seize him in this "hour" (12:27), Jesus embraces the prospect of suffering as the "hour" when he will pass out of this world to his heavenly Father (13:1). His disciples, too, will share in this trial as the "hour" strikes them with the fear and distress of a woman in labor (16:21-22). At the historical level, then, the "hour" is the time when Christ passes through the agonies of betrayal and bodily torment, finally mounting the Cross out of love for the Father and as a sacrifice for our salvation. This "hour" of Christ's humiliation and death is in John's Gospel the "hour" of his exaltation that becomes the source of everlasting life for the world.

THE LITURGICAL HOUR

If Christ's "hour" is linked with the historical events of his Passion, it also reaches beyond them into the liturgical commemoration of these events in the life of the Church. Several statements regarding the "hour" of Jesus are thus connected with Christian worship.

1. In Jn 2:4, Jesus responds to his Mother's request for wine with the puzzling statement "My hour has not yet come." The hidden premise, it seems, is that when this still-distant "hour" finally arrives, he expects to provide an abundance of the finest wine (2:10). This may be read as an allusion to the liturgy, where believers all over the world gather to worship Christ as he pours himself into the eucharistic cup under the visible sign of wine.

2. In Jn 4:21-23, Jesus insists that his coming "hour" has everything to do with worship—and not just with any worship, but with a spiritual adoration of the Father superior to any previously known in Samaria or even in Israel! The worship characteristic of this "hour" will not be confined to any particular mountain sanctuary, but will lift true worshipers up to a new and heavenly height in the Spirit (Rev 1:10, chaps. 4 and 5).

3. In Jn 5:25-29, Jesus looks to his "hour" as a time when those who are dead will hear his voice and live again. This, too, has connections with the liturgy, where Christ continues to speak through the Scriptures and awaken souls deadened by sin.

4. Finally, Christ's "hour" will bring in a harvest of believers from every nation, because Jesus, like a grain of wheat that dies and is buried in the earth, enables Israel and every nation to sprout into new life (12:20-24). This blessing comes not only through Christ's death, but also through his risen and glorified humanity, which is the wheat that becomes for us the "bread of life" in the Eucharist (6:48).

These two dimensions of the "hour" are part of the one Paschal Mystery of Christ. We cannot, therefore, drive a wedge between the historical and the liturgical, between the *sacrificial* gift of Christ to the Father on the Cross and the *sacramental* gift of Christ to us in the liturgy. This was recognized in the early Church, where the "hour" of Jesus referred not only to his suffering and death, but, as in the ancient liturgies of St. James and St. Mark, the expression "this hour" referred to re-presentation of the Passion in the eucharistic celebration.

Combined with references to Baptism (3:5), the Eucharist (6:35-58), and Reconciliation (20:23), we see in John's Gospel that the "hour" of Jesus that unfolds during Holy Week also extends throughout the centuries and throughout the world as Christians commemorate the sacred mysteries of this "hour" in the sacramental liturgy of the New Covenant. «

him." [53]The father knew that was the hour when Jesus had said to him, "Your son will live"; and he himself believed, and all his household. [54]This was now the second sign that Jesus did when he had come from Judea to Galilee.

Jesus Heals on the Sabbath

5 After this there was a feast of the Jews, and Jesus went up to Jerusalem.

2 Now there is in Jerusalem by the Sheep Gate a pool, in Hebrew called Beth-za´tha,[j] which has five porticoes. [3]In these lay a multitude of invalids, blind, lame, paralyzed.[k] [5]One man was there, who had been ill for thirty-eight years. [6]When Jesus saw him and knew that he had been lying there a long time, he said to him, "Do you want to be healed?" [7]The sick man answered him, "Sir, I have no man to put me into the pool when the water is troubled, and while I am going another steps down before me." [8]Jesus said to him, "Rise, take up your pallet, and walk." [9]And at once the man was healed, and he took up his pallet and walked.

Now that day was the sabbath. [10]So the Jews said to the man who was cured, "It is the sabbath, it is not lawful for you to carry your pallet." [11]But he answered them, "The man who healed me said to me, 'Take up your pallet, and walk.' " [12]They asked him, "Who is the man who said to you, 'Take up your pallet, and walk'?" [13]Now the man who had been healed did not know who it was, for Jesus had

withdrawn, as there was a crowd in the place. [14]Afterward, Jesus found him in the temple, and said to him, "See, you are well! Sin no more, that nothing worse befall you." [15]The man went away and told the Jews that it was Jesus who had healed him. [16]And this was why the Jews persecuted Jesus, because he did this on the sabbath. [17]But Jesus answered them, "My Father is working still, and I am working." [18]This was why the Jews sought all the more to kill him, because he not only broke the sabbath but also called God his Father, making himself equal with God.

The Authority of the Son

19 Jesus said to them, "Truly, truly, I say to you, the Son can do nothing of his own accord, but only what he sees the Father doing; for whatever he does, that the Son does likewise. [20]For the Father loves the Son, and shows him all that he himself is doing; and greater works than these will he show him, that you may marvel. [21]For as the Father raises the dead and gives them life, so also the Son gives life to whom he will. [22]The Father judges no one, but has given all judgment to the Son, [23]that all may honor the Son, even as they honor the Father. He who does not honor the Son does not honor the Father who sent him. [24]Truly, truly, I say to you, he who hears my word and believes him who sent me, has eternal life; he does not come into judgment, but has passed from death to life.

4:53: Acts 11:14.   **4:54:** Jn 2:11.   **5:2:** Neh 3:1; 12:39.   **5:8:** Mk 2:11; Mt 9:6; Lk 5:24.   **5:10:** Neh 13:19; Jer 17:21; Jn 7:23; 9:16; Mk 2:24.   **5:14:** Mk 2:5.   **5:17:** Gen 2:3.   **5:18:** Jn 7:1; 10:33.   **5:19:** Jn 5:30; 8:28; 14:10.   **5:20:** Jn 14:12.   **5:21:** Rom 4:17; 8:11; Jn 11:25.   **5:23:** Lk 10:16; 1 Jn 2:23.   **5:24:** Jn 3:18.

4:54 the second sign: Despite numerous signs performed in Jerusalem (2:23), this is only the second performed in Galilee (2:11). See word study: *Signs* at Jn 2:11.

5:1 a feast of the Jews: John usually identifies the religious festivals that Jesus attends, whether it is Passover (2:13), Tabernacles (7:2), or Dedication (10:22). Here the unnamed feast may be Pentecost (Weeks), which celebrates the spring harvest as well as the giving of the Torah to Israel. It is one of three pilgrim feasts that required Israelite men to travel to Jerusalem (Deut 16:16; 2 Chron 8:13) (CCC 583).

5:2 the Sheep Gate: An entryway in the northeastern wall of Jerusalem used in bringing sheep to the Temple for sacrifice (Neh 3:1). Two pools were built in the same area of the city; they were surrounded by four colonnade walkways and separated by a fifth portico running between them. One of these pools was called **Bethzatha** and was believed to possess healing properties.

5:5 thirty-eight years: The man's protracted suffering is evident to Jesus (5:6). • The duration of the man's illness, due to some unspecified sin (5:14), recalls the duration of Israel's wandering in the wilderness after rebelling against Yahweh at Kadesh (Num 13:25—14:11). The grueling journey from Kadesh to the threshold of Canaan lasted 38 years (Deut 2:14).

5:8 Rise . . . and walk: According to Jewish tradition, medical attention could be given on the Sabbath only when some-

one's life was in danger. The boldness of Jesus in neglecting this convention reflects his own theological stance that giving rest to suffering souls, whether or not they are on the brink of death, fulfills the true intent of the Sabbath (CCC 2173). See note on Lk 6:1.

5:13 Jesus had withdrawn: i.e., from the man just cured of paralysis. • *Morally* (St. Cyril of Jerusalem, *Sermon on the Paralytic* 16), Jesus disappears into the crowd to teach us to shun worldly praise. Though we are inclined to boast of our accomplishments, or at least want to be recognized for them, humility must turn us away from whatever acclaim might lead us to pride.

5:14 Sin no more: The Bible reveals a link between sin and suffering, with the former being the cause of the latter (Ps 107:17). This general truth, however, does not extend to every individual case (9:3).

5:17 My Father is working: God the Son imitates God the Father and obeys all that he hears from him (5:19–21). Jesus thus depicts himself as the apprentice of Yahweh, drawing on the familiar custom of sons learning by observation and imitation the trade skills of their fathers.

5:18 equal with God: By calling God his Father, Jesus claims a status of divine Sonship for himself. • The three Persons of the Trinity equally possess the same fullness of divine life and Being. Although the Son is less than the Father in his humanity (14:28), he is equal to the Father in his divinity (10:33) (CCC 253–54).

5:24 from death to life: Signifies a spiritual transfer from the curses of the Old Covenant to the blessing of the New (Deut 30:15–20; Eph 2:1–5). Believers are rescued from the fallen family of Adam and reinstated in the divine family of God (Rom 5:12–21) (CCC 580, 1470).

---

[j] Other ancient authorities read *Bethesda*, others *Bethsaida*.
[k] Other ancient authorities insert, wholly or in part, *waiting for the moving of the water;* [4]*for an angel of the Lord went down at certain seasons into the pool, and troubled the water; whoever stepped in first after the troubling of the water was healed of whatever disease he had.*

25 "Truly, truly, I say to you, the hour is coming, and now is, when the dead will hear the voice of the Son of God, and those who hear will live. [26]For as the Father has life in himself, so he has granted the Son also to have life in himself, [27]and has given him authority to execute judgment, because he is the Son of man. [28]Do not marvel at this; for the hour is coming when all who are in the tombs will hear his voice [29]and come forth, those who have done good, to the resurrection of life, and those who have done evil, to the resurrection of judgment.

The Testimony to Jesus

30 "I can do nothing on my own authority; as I hear, I judge; and my judgment is just, because I seek not my own will but the will of him who sent me. [31]If I bear witness to myself, my testimony is not true; [32]there is another who bears witness to me, and I know that the testimony which he bears to me is true. [33]You sent to John, and he has borne witness to the truth. [34]Not that the testimony which I receive is from man; but I say this that you may be saved. [35]He was a burning and shining lamp, and you were willing to rejoice for a while in his light. [36]But the testimony which I have is greater than that of John; for the works which the Father has granted me to accomplish, these very works which I am doing, bear me witness that the Father has sent me. [37]And the Father who sent me has himself borne witness to me. His voice you have never heard, his form you have never seen; [38]and you do not have his word abiding in you, for you do not believe him whom he has sent. [39]You search the Scriptures, because you think that in them you have eternal life; and it is they that bear witness to me; [40]yet you refuse to come to me that you may have life. [41]I do not receive glory from men. [42]But I know that you have not the love of God within you. [43]I have come in my Father's name, and you do not receive me; if another comes in his own name, him you will receive. [44]How can you believe, who receive glory from one another and do not seek the glory that comes from the only God? [45]Do not think that I shall accuse you to the Father; it is Moses who accuses you, on whom you set your hope. [46]If you believed Moses, you would believe me, for he wrote of me. [47]But if you do not believe his writings, how will you believe my words?"

Feeding the Five Thousand

6 After this Jesus went to the other side of the Sea of Galilee, which is the Sea of Tibe´ri-as. [2]And a multitude followed him, because they saw the signs which he did on those who were diseased. [3]Jesus went up into the hills, and there sat down with his disciples. [4]Now the Passover, the feast of the Jews, was at hand. [5]Lifting up his eyes, then, and seeing that a multitude was coming to him, Jesus said to Philip, "How are we to buy bread, so

---

5:25: Jn 4:21; 16:2, 32.　5:29: Dan 12:2; Acts 24:15; Jn 11:24; Mt 25:46; 1 Cor 15:52.　5:30: Jn 5:19; 8:16; 6:38.
5:31–37: Jn 8:14–18.　5:33: Jn 1:7, 19.　5:34: 1 Jn 5:9.　5:36: Jn 10:25; 14:11; 15:24; Mt 11:4.
5:39: Lk 24:27; Acts 13:27.　5:43: Mt 24:5.　5:45: Jn 9:28; Rom 2:17.　5:47: Lk 16:29, 31.
6:1–13: Mt 14:13–21; Mk 6:32–44; Lk 9:10–17.　6:5: Jn 1:43; 12:21.

5:26 life in himself: The Father is the first link in a chain of supernatural life, since he alone has not received divine life from anyone else. His capacity to give life, however, is shared by Christ, who receives life from the Father and gives it to the world through the sacraments (6:53; 10:10).

5:27 execute judgment: The Son is given absolute sovereignty over life and death, being authorized by the Father to judge the living and the dead and decide their eternal destiny (Mt 25:31–46; Acts 10:42; CCC 679).

5:29 the resurrection: Christ claims the authority to raise all men from death, the righteous and wicked alike (Acts 24:15). ● Two oracles from the OT stand in the background of Jesus' teaching. (1) Dan 12:2 envisions a final separation of saints and sinners once their bodies have awakened from the sleep of bodily death. (2) Ezek 37:1–4 envisions the resurrection, where bones and flesh are reassembled and made to live again. Rising from the grave is made possible by the spoken words of Ezekiel, called the Son of man, and the life-giving breath of the Spirit. Jesus casts himself in the lead role of these prophetic narratives: he is the "Son of man" (5:27) whose powerful "voice" (5:25) raises the dead from their "tombs" (5:28) and separates them for everlasting "life" or eternal "judgment" (5:29) (CCC 997–1001).

5:30–47 Jewish legal tradition required two or three witnesses to sustain a claim in court (Deut 19:15). Jesus has a list of witnesses beyond the required number: (1) John the Baptist (5:33), (2) his miracles (5:36), (3) the Father (5:37), (4) the Scriptures (5:39), (5) and Moses (5:46) all bear witness to his divine authority and mission.

5:35 burning and shining lamp: The ministry of John the Baptist lights the way for Israel to see and accept its Mes-

siah (1:31). ● Elijah is similarly depicted as a fiery torch in Sir 48:1. See note on 1:21.

5:46 he wrote of me: Jesus follows the Jewish tradition that Moses authored the Pentateuch (Gen—Deut). Moses thus described the Messiah as a Redeemer (Gen 3:15), a universal King (Gen 49:10), and a Prophet like himself (Deut 18:15–19).

6:1–14 The multiplication of the loaves is the only miracle, besides the Resurrection, that is recorded in all four Gospels. John's account forms the preface to Jesus' extensive discourse on the "bread of life" in 6:35–59. ● The two food miracles in John involve bread (6:1–14) and wine (2:1–11). Together they anticipate the eucharistic liturgy, where Jesus gives himself as food under the visible signs of bread and wine (CCC 1335).

6:1 Sea of Tiberias: Also known as the "Sea of Galilee" (Mk 1:16) or the "lake of Gennesaret" (Lk 5:1). The city of Tiberias, then the administrative capital of Galilee, was built by Herod Antipas on its western shore about A.D. 20 in honor of the Roman emperor Tiberius Caesar.

6:4 the Passover: Three times this feast is mentioned in John (2:13; 11:55). It was celebrated annually in Jerusalem to commemorate Israel's deliverance from Egyptian slavery (Ex 12). Central to the feast is a liturgical meal, called a seder, in which the story of the Exodus is retold, psalms are sung, and a lamb is eaten with unleavened bread and other condiments. The evangelist mentions this upcoming feast to hint that Jesus will give new and greater meaning to the Passover. He is the true "Lamb of God" (1:29), whose redeeming work will accomplish a new deliverance from the slavery of sin (8:31–36) in a sacramental and liturgical meal (6:53–58; 1 Cor 5:7–8). The significance of

that these people may eat?" [6]This he said to test him, for he himself knew what he would do. [7]Philip answered him, "Two hundred denarii[*l*] would not buy enough bread for each of them to get a little." [8]One of his disciples, Andrew, Simon Peter's brother, said to him, [9]"There is a lad here who has five barley loaves and two fish; but what are they among so many?" [10]Jesus said, "Make the people sit down." Now there was much grass in the place; so the men sat down, in number about five thousand. [11]Jesus then took the loaves, and when he had given thanks, he distributed them to those who were seated; so also the fish, as much as they wanted. [12]And when they had eaten their fill, he told his disciples, "Gather up the fragments left over, that nothing may be lost." [13]So they gathered them up and filled twelve baskets with fragments from the five barley loaves, left by those who had eaten. [14]When the people saw the sign which he had done, they said, "This is indeed the prophet who is to come into the world!"

15 Perceiving then that they were about to come and take him by force to make him king, Jesus withdrew again to the hills by himself.

Jesus Walks on the Sea

16 When evening came, his disciples went down to the sea, [17]got into a boat, and started across the sea to Caper′na-um. It was now dark, and Jesus had not yet come to them. [18]The sea rose because a strong wind was blowing. [19]When they had rowed about three or four miles,[*m*] they saw Jesus walking on the sea and drawing near to the boat. They were frightened, [20]but he said to them, "It is I; do not be afraid." [21]Then they were glad to take him into the boat, and immediately the boat was at the land to which they were going.

The Bread from Heaven

22 On the next day the people who remained on the other side of the sea saw that there had been only one boat there, and that Jesus had not entered the boat with his disciples, but that his disciples had gone away alone. [23]However, boats from Tibe′ri-as came near the place where they ate the bread after the Lord had given thanks. [24]So when the people saw that Jesus was not there, nor his disciples, they themselves got into the boats and went to Caper′na-um, seeking Jesus.

25 When they found him on the other side of the sea, they said to him, "Rabbi, when did you come here?" [26]Jesus answered them, "Truly, truly, I say to you, you seek me, not because you saw signs, but because you ate your fill of the loaves. [27]Do not labor for the food which perishes, but for the food which endures to eternal life, which the Son of man will give to you; for on him has God the Father set his seal." [28]Then they said to him, "What must we do, to be doing the works of God?" [29]Jesus answered them, "This is the work of God, that you believe in him whom he has sent." [30]So they said to him, "Then what sign do you do, that we may see, and believe you? What work do you perform? [31]Our fathers ate the manna in the wilderness; as it is

---

6:8: Jn 1:40; 12:22.   **6:9:** Jn 21:9–13.   **6:14:** Mt 21:11.   **6:15:** Jn 6:3; 18:36.   **6:16–21:** Mt 14:22–27; Mk 6:45–51.   **6:27:** Is 55:2.   **6:29:** 1 Thess 1:3; 1 Jn 3:23.   **6:30:** Mt 12:38; Mk 8:11.   **6:31:** Ex 16:4, 15; Num 11:8; Neh 9:15; Ps 78:24; 105:40.

Passover, here placed in the background of John 6, will move to the foreground when Jesus transforms this feast into the memorial meal of the New Covenant at the Last Supper (Mt 26:17–29; CCC 1340). See note on 19:36.

6:7 Two hundred denarii: About 200 days' wages for a laborer (Mt 20:2).

6:9 barley loaves: The food of the poor. • This detail recalls the similar miracle of Elisha, who multiplied 20 loaves of barley for 100 men with some left over (2 Kings 4:42–44). The miracle of Jesus is comparatively greater: he begins with fewer loaves (5), multiplies them for a larger crowd (5,000), and likewise has bread left over (6:13). • Allegorically (St. Bede, *Hom. in Evan.*), the five loaves are the five books of the Torah, the two fish are the Prophets and Psalms, and the young boy is the Jewish people. When Jesus receives these OT Scriptures from the Jews, he breaks open their deeper, spiritual meanings to refresh the multitudes.

6:11 given thanks: Renders the Greek verb *eucharisteō*, from which the English word "Eucharist" is derived. The miracle of the loaves thus foreshadows the institution of this sacrament at the Last Supper. See note on Mk 6:35–44.

6:14 the prophet: i.e., the messianic prophet foretold by Moses. See note on 1:21.

6:15 make him king: Israel hoped for a militant Messiah to overthrow the Romans and reestablish their national independence in Palestine. Jesus backs away from these aspirations,

knowing that his kingdom is heavenly and spiritual (CCC 439). See note on 18:36.

6:20 It is I: Or "I am". • The reassurance that Jesus gives to the disciples is also an act of self-revelation. His words recall the holy name "I AM" that Yahweh revealed to Moses at the burning bush (Ex 3:14). The claim to divinity inherent in this name is substantiated by Jesus' exhibition of power over the laws of nature (6:19; Job 9:8). Several times Jesus claims this divine name for himself in the Fourth Gospel (8:24, 58; 13:19; 18:6) (CCC 213). **do not be afraid:** Words often spoken when God reveals himself to his people, whether directly or through an angel (Gen 26:24; Judg 6:22–23; Lk 1:30).

6:23 from Tiberias: i.e., from the western shore of the Sea of Galilee. See note on 6:1.

6:25 Rabbi: A Hebrew title for respected Jewish teachers (1:38).

6:27 food which perishes: Earthly food is necessary to sustain earthly life, but because it is perishable it does not suffice to give us supernatural life or to safeguard against death (6:49). Only Christ can give us food that satisfies our spiritual hunger and gives everlasting life. The subsequent narrative will identify this heavenly food as the Eucharist (6:50–58).

6:31 He gave them bread: A reference to Ex 16:4. • Jesus is challenged to match the provision of manna by Moses. He responds by stressing that although the manna had a heavenly origin (6:32), it did not bring the Israelites to their heavenly destiny (6:49). Manna is rather a food that perishes, since it melted away every morning (Ex 16:21) and turned foul if it was stored overnight (Ex 16:19–20).

[*l*] The denarius was a day's wage for a laborer.
[*m*] Greek *twenty-five or thirty stadia.*

written, 'He gave them bread from heaven to eat.' " [32]Jesus then said to them, "Truly, truly, I say to you, it was not Moses who gave you the bread from heaven; my Father gives you the true bread from heaven. [33]For the bread of God is that which comes down from heaven, and gives life to the world." [34]They said to him, "Lord, give us this bread always."

35 Jesus said to them, "I am the bread of life; he who comes to me shall not hunger, and he who believes in me shall never thirst. [36]But I said to you that you have seen me and yet do not believe. [37]All that the Father gives me will come to me; and him who comes to me I will not cast out. [38]For I have come down from heaven, not to do my own will, but the will of him who sent me; [39]and this is the will of him who sent me, that I should lose nothing of all that he has given me, but raise it up at the last day. [40]For this is the will of my Father, that every one who sees the Son and believes in him should have eternal life; and I will raise him up at the last day."

41 The Jews then murmured at him, because he said, "I am the bread which came down from heaven." [42]They said, "Is not this Jesus, the son of Joseph, whose father and mother we know? How does he now say, 'I have come down from heaven'?" [43]Jesus answered them, "Do not murmur among yourselves. [44]No one can come to me unless the Father who sent me draws him; and I will raise him up at the last day. [45]It is written in the prophets, 'And they shall all be taught by God.' Every one who has heard and learned from the Father comes to me. [46]Not that any one has seen the Father except him who is from God; he has seen the Father. [47]Truly, truly, I say to you, he who believes has eternal life. [48]I am the bread of life. [49]Your fathers ate the manna in the wilderness, and they died. [50]This is the bread which comes down from heaven, that a man may eat of it and not die. [51]I am the living bread which came down from heaven; if any one eats of this bread, he will live for ever; and the bread which I shall give for the life of the world is my flesh."

52 The Jews then disputed among themselves, saying, "How can this man give us his flesh to eat?" [53]So Jesus said to them, "Truly, truly, I say to you, unless you eat the flesh of the Son of man and drink his blood, you have no life in you; [54]he who eats my flesh and drinks my blood has eternal life, and I will raise him up at the last day. [55]For my flesh is food indeed, and my blood is drink indeed. [56]He who eats my flesh and drinks my blood abides in me, and I in him. [57]As the living Father sent me, and I live because of the Father, so he who eats me will live because of me.

6:34: Jn 4:15; Mt 6:11.   **6:35:** Jn 6:48–50; 4:14.   **6:37:** Jn 17:2.   **6:38:** Jn 4:34; 5:30.   **6:39:** Jn 17:12; 18:9.   **6:40:** Jn 5:29; 11:24; 6:54.   **6:42:** Lk 4:22; Jn 7:27.   **6:44:** Jer 31:3; Hos 11:4; Jn 12:32; 6:65.   **6:45:** 1 Thess 4:9; 1 Jn 2:27; Is 54:13.   **6:46:** Jn 1:18.   **6:52:** Jn 3:4; 4:9.   **6:56:** Jn 15:4; 1 Jn 3:24; 4:15.   **6:58:** Jn 6:41, 51.

6:32 the true bread: The wilderness manna was not false bread; it was merely a sign of the imperishable eucharistic bread that the Father sends down from heaven in Jesus (6:51; CCC 1094).

6:35–59 The Bread of Life discourse. Interpretations of this sermon often take one of two positions. Some think of the discourse as an extensive invitation to faith, so that eating the bread of life is seen as a metaphor for believing in Jesus. Others interpret the discourse along sacramental lines, so that eating the bread of life means partaking of the Eucharist. Both of these views are true and can be correlated with a natural and symmetrical division of the sermon into two parts. (1) *Invitation to Faith* (6:35–47). The first half of the discourse opens with the statement "I am the bread of life" (6:35). This is followed by a string of invitations to come to Jesus and believe in him for salvation. The metaphorical import of Jesus' teaching is so obvious that it stands out in the response of the Jews, who ask him, not why he calls himself bread, but how he can claim to have descended from heaven (6:42). (2) *Invitation to the Eucharist* (6:48–58). The second half of the discourse likewise opens with the statement "I am the bread of life" (6:48). This is followed by a string of invitations to eat the flesh of Jesus and drink his blood. Here the literal import of Jesus' teaching is so obvious that it, too, stands out in the response of the Jews, who ask how it is possible to consume his flesh (6:52). In the end, these two halves of the sermon work in tandem, since without faith we can neither be united with Christ nor recognize his presence in the Eucharist. If eating is believing in 6:35–47, then believing leads to eating in 6:48–58 (CCC 161, 1381).

6:37 All that the Father gives: Alludes to the mystery of predestination. See note on Rom 8:29.

6:38 not . . . my own will: The human will of Jesus and the divine will of the Father are in such perfect harmony that there is never any tension or competition between them (4:34; 8:29; Mk 14:36; CCC 475, 2824).

6:41 Jews then murmured: Recalls how the Israelites complained against the Lord and Moses in the wilderness (Ex 16:2; 17:2–3; Num 11:1).

6:45 taught by God: A paraphrase of Is 54:13. ● Isaiah envisions the messianic age as a time when Yahweh will restore, prosper, and teach the children of Israel. Other passages, such as Jer 31:34, may be included in Jesus' broad reference to the **prophets**.

6:51 I shall give: The future tense points both to the Cross, where Jesus surrenders his life for human sins, and to the eucharistic liturgy, where Jesus offers himself as living bread to a starving world.

6:52 his flesh to eat?: The crowd is thinking of cannibalism, i.e., the sin of eating a human corpse, an idea thoroughly repugnant to them (Deut 28:53). This is a misunderstanding. Jesus gives us, not his mortal flesh as it was during his earthly ministry, but his glorified humanity as it was after rising from the dead. This is why he calls himself the "living bread" (6:51).

6:53 eat the flesh . . . drink his blood: Jesus is speaking literally and sacramentally. If he were speaking metaphorically or figuratively, his words would echo a Hebrew idiom where consuming flesh and blood refers to the brutalities of war (Deut 32:42; Ezek 39:17–18). **no life in you:** i.e., divine life. ● Drinking the blood of animals is forbidden under the Old Covenant (Gen 9:4; Lev 17:10–13; Deut 12:16). To do so is to consume "life" that is merely natural and of a lower order than human life. Jesus' injunction does not fall under these prohibitions. The "life" he imparts is not natural but supernatural; it does not pull us down to the level of animals, it elevates us to become sharers in his divine nature (2 Pet 1:4) (CCC 1391).

[58]This is the bread which came down from heaven, not such as the fathers ate and died; he who eats this bread will live for ever." [59]This he said in the synagogue, as he taught at Caper′na-um.

The Words of Eternal Life

60 Many of his disciples, when they heard it, said, "This is a hard saying; who can listen to it?" [61]But Jesus, knowing in himself that his disciples murmured at it, said to them, "Do you take offense at this? [62]Then what if you were to see the Son of man ascending where he was before? [63]It is the spirit that gives life, the flesh is of no avail; the words that I have spoken to you are spirit and life. [64]But there are some of you that do not believe." For Jesus knew from the first who those were that did not believe, and who it was that would betray him. [65]And he said, "This is why I told you that no one can come to me unless it is granted him by the Father."

66 After this many of his disciples drew back and no longer walked with him. [67]Jesus said to the Twelve, "Will you also go away?" [68]Simon Peter answered him, "Lord, to whom shall we go? You have the words of eternal life; [69]and we have believed, and have come to know, that you are the Holy One of God." [70]Jesus answered them, "Did I not choose you, the Twelve, and one of you is a devil?" [71]He spoke of Judas the son of Simon Iscariot, for he, one of the Twelve, was to betray him.

The Unbelief of Jesus' Brethren

7 After this Jesus went about in Galilee; he would not go about in Judea, because the Jews[n] sought to kill him. [2]Now the Jews' feast of Tabernacles was at hand. [3]So his brethren said to him, "Leave here and go to Judea, that your disciples may see the works you are doing. [4]For no man works in secret if he seeks to be known openly. If you do these things, show yourself to the world." [5]For even his brethren did not believe in him. [6]Jesus said to them, "My time has not yet come, but your time is always here. [7]The world cannot hate you, but it hates me because I testify of it that its works are evil. [8]Go to the feast yourselves; I am not[o] going up

---

6:59: Jn 6:25.   6:61: Mt 11:6.   6:62: Jn 3:13; 17:5.   6:63: 2 Cor 3:6; Jn 6:68.   6:64: Jn 2:25.   6:65: Jn 6:44; 3:27.
6:68–69: Mk 8:27–30.   6:70: Jn 15:16, 19.   6:71: Jn 13:2, 27; 17:12.   7:2: Lev 23:34; Deut 16:16.
7:3: Mk 3:21, 31; Mt 12:46.   7:6: Mt 26:18; Jn 2:4; 7:30.   7:7: Jn 15:18–21.

6:58 will live for ever: The expression occurs rarely in the Bible, only twice in John (6:51, 58) and once in the Greek version of Gen 3:22. • A comparison is thus implied between the Tree of Life, which bore the fruit of immortality, and the Bread of Life, which tradition calls the "medicine of immortality" (CCC 1331).

6:62 the Son of man: The heavenly figure described in Dan 7:13. See topical essay: *Jesus, the Son of Man* at Lk 17.

6:63 the spirit . . . the flesh: A contrast between the Spirit's ability to enlighten our minds (14:26) and human reason's inability to comprehend revealed truths apart from faith (8:15). It is this earthbound perspective that is profitless in the face of divine mysteries. Note that Jesus is not speaking of his own "flesh", which does in fact give life to the world (6:51; Eph 2:13–16; Heb 10:10) (CCC 737).

6:66 his disciples drew back: This is the only instance in the Gospels where followers of Jesus abandon him in such large numbers. Even so, Jesus still makes no effort to soften his words or clear up potential misunderstandings about his eucharistic teaching (CCC 1336).

6:69 the Holy One: A title for Jesus also in Mk 1:24, Lk 4:34, and Acts 3:14. Here it is a confession of faith by Peter, who believes the words of Christ from the heart, even though his head does not yet understand the mysteries revealed in the discourse (6:35–58).

6:71 Judas: Anticipates the defection of the betrayer during the Last Supper (13:21–30).

7:2 feast of Tabernacles: Also called the "feast of Booths" (Lev 23:33–43; Deut 16:13–16). It is a seven-day fall festival held annually in Jerusalem. The feast of Tabernacles commemorates both the completion of the autumn harvest and Yahweh's provisions for Israel during their Exodus journey through the wilderness. Throughout the week, Jewish pilgrims dwelled in small huts made of tree branches called "booths". Two liturgical ceremonies from this feast hang as a backdrop behind Jesus' teaching in chaps. 7 and 8. (1) Each morning Levitical priests drew water from the pool of Siloam in the southern quarter of Jerusalem, carried it in procession into the Temple, and poured it out as a libation next to the altar of sacrifice. This is connected with Jesus' teaching about "water" in 7:37–39. (2) Giant cande-

labras burned in the sanctuary (Court of Women) that illuminated the Temple courts; at the same time dancers with flaming torches processed through the Temple amid singing and music. This is linked with Jesus' teaching about "light" in 8:12.

7:3 his brethren: Close relatives of Jesus, but not biological siblings. Although lacking in faith here, they later become believers (Acts 1:14). See note on Mt 12:46.

7:6 My time: Jesus is not scheduled to manifest the fullness of his glory until the "hour" of his Passion (7:30; 13:1). His earthly relatives, therefore, cannot dictate the timing or direction of his heavenly mission.

7:7 The world: i.e., the family of sinful man. The relatives of Jesus are still part of the world because they are not hated by it as he is (15:18–19). See note on 1:10.

7:8 I am not going up: The expression has two levels of meaning: (1) It is not yet time for Jesus to travel up to Jerusalem,

WORD STUDY

Eats (6:54)

Trōgō (Gk.): A verb meaning "chew" or "gnaw". It is used five times in the Fourth Gospel and only once elsewhere in the NT. Greek literature used it to describe the feeding of animals such as mules, pigs, and cattle, and in some cases for human eating. In John, the verb is used four times in the second half of the Bread of Life discourse (Jn 6:54, 56, 57, 58). This marks a noticeable shift in Jesus' teaching, which up until 6:54 made use of a more common verb for eating (Gk. *esthiō*, 6:49, 50, 51, 53). The change in vocabulary marks a change of focus and emphasis, from the necessity of faith to the consumption of the Eucharist. The graphic and almost crude connotation of this verb thus adds greater force to the repetition of his words: he demands we express our faith by eating, in a real and physical way, his life-giving flesh in the sacrament.

---

[n] Or *Judeans*.   [o] Other ancient authorities add *yet*.

to this feast, for my time has not yet fully come."
⁹So saying, he remained in Galilee.

Jesus at the Feast of Tabernacles

10 But after his brethren had gone up to the feast, then he also went up, not publicly but in private. ¹¹The Jews were looking for him at the feast, and saying, "Where is he?" ¹²And there was much muttering about him among the people. While some said, "He is a good man," others said, "No, he is leading the people astray." ¹³Yet for fear of the Jews no one spoke openly of him.

14 About the middle of the feast Jesus went up into the temple and taught. ¹⁵The Jews marveled at it, saying, "How is it that this man has learning,ᵇ when he has never studied?" ¹⁶So Jesus answered them, "My teaching is not mine, but his who sent me; ¹⁷if any man's will is to do his will, he shall know whether the teaching is from God or whether I am speaking on my own authority. ¹⁸He who speaks on his own authority seeks his own glory; but he who seeks the glory of him who sent him is true, and in him there is no falsehood. ¹⁹Did not Moses give you the law? Yet none of you keeps the law. Why do you seek to kill me?" ²⁰The people answered, "You have a demon! Who is seeking to kill you?" ²¹Jesus answered them, "I did one deed, and you all marvel at it. ²²Moses gave you circumcision (not that it is from Moses, but from the fathers), and you circumcise a man upon the sabbath. ²³If on the sabbath a man receives circumcision, so that the law of Moses may not be broken, are you angry with me because on the sabbath I made a man's whole body well? ²⁴Do not judge by appearances, but judge with right judgment."

Is This the Christ?

25 Some of the people of Jerusalem therefore said, "Is not this the man whom they seek to kill? ²⁶And here he is, speaking openly, and they say nothing to him! Can it be that the authorities really know that this is the Christ? ²⁷Yet we know where this man comes from; and when the Christ appears, no one will know where he comes from." ²⁸So Jesus proclaimed, as he taught in the temple, "You know me, and you know where I come from? But I have not come of my own accord; he who sent me is true, and him you do not know. ²⁹I know him, for I come from him, and he sent me." ³⁰So they sought to arrest him; but no one laid hands on him, because his hour had not yet come. ³¹Yet many of the people believed in him; they said, "When the Christ appears, will he do more signs than this man has done?"

Officers Are Sent to Arrest Jesus

32 The Pharisees heard the crowd thus muttering about him, and the chief priests and Pharisees sent officers to arrest him. ³³Jesus then said, "I shall be with you a little longer, and then I go to him who sent me; ³⁴you will seek me and you will not find me; where I am you cannot come." ³⁵The Jews said to one another, "Where does this man intend to go that we shall not find him? Does he intend to go to the Dispersion among the Greeks and teach the Greeks? ³⁶What does he mean by saying, 'You will seek me and you will not find me,' and, 'Where I am you cannot come'?"

Rivers of Living Water

37 On the last day of the feast, the great day, Jesus stood up and proclaimed, "If any one thirst,

---

7:12: Jn 7:40–43.   **7:13:** Jn 19:38; 20:19.   **7:19:** Jn 1:17.   **7:20:** Jn 8:48; 10:20; Mt 11:18; Mk 3:22.   **7:21:** Jn 5:2–9.
   7:22: Lev 12:3; Gen 17:10; 21:4.   **7:23:** Mk 3:5; Lk 13:12; 14:4.   **7:24:** Jn 8:15; Is 11:3; Zech 7:9.   **7:27:** Jn 6:42; 7:41; 9:29.
   7:28: Jn 8:42.   **7:29:** Jn 8:55; 17:25; Mt 11:27.   **7:30:** Jn 7:44; 10:39; Mk 12:12; Jn 8:20.   **7:31:** Jn 8:30; 10:42; 11:45.
   7:33: Jn 8:21; 12:35; 13:33; 14:19; 16:16–19.   **7:35:** Jas 1:1; 1 Pet 1:1; Jn 12:20; Acts 11:20.   **7:37:** Lev 23:36; Jn 4:10, 14.

---

(2) nor is it time for him to ascend in glory to the Father (20:17).

7:13 fear of the Jews: Rumors had leaked out that the Jerusalem authorities were plotting against Jesus (7:1, 11, 19). The crowds were thus reluctant to be associated with him or his teaching.

7:14 middle of the feast: Either the third or fourth day of the week-long festival. See note on 7:2.

7:15 never studied: Jewish students were normally tutored by older rabbis in the interpretation of Scripture and in the traditions of their revered teachers. Jesus exhibits such profound insight into Scripture and spiritual things that many are shocked that he has no formal training (Mk 6:1–3; Lk 2:47).

7:18 the glory of him: i.e., of his heavenly Father (5:44; 17:5).

7:21 I did one deed: The healing of the lame man in 5:1–9.

7:22 circumcision: A sign of the Abrahamic covenant (Gen 17:10–14) that was later incorporated into the Mosaic covenant (Lev 12:3). According to Jewish tradition, the duty to circumcise newborn boys on the eighth day overrides the duty to observe the Sabbath rest when it falls on the same day. Jesus reasons that if *part* of the body may be lawfully tended to, then how much more should the *whole* body participate in

the blessings of the covenant on the Sabbath (7:23) (CCC 2173).

7:26 the authorities: Probably members of the Sanhedrin in Jerusalem. See note on Mk 14:55.

7:27 no one will know: Two traditions regarding the birth and origin of the Messiah circulated in ancient Judaism. (1) Some expected the Messiah to grow up in obscurity and be manifested to the world only as an adult. (2) Others expected the Messiah to come from Bethlehem in accordance with the prophecy of Mic 5:2. The irony here is that both are true of Jesus: his heavenly origin in the Trinity is unknown to his audience (8:14), as is his birth in Bethlehem (Lk 2:4–7).

7:30 his hour: See topical essay: *The "Hour" of Jesus* at Jn 4.

7:32 officers: Temple police in Jerusalem (Acts 4:1–3; 5:24–26).

7:35 Dispersion among the Greeks: i.e., among the Jews and Gentiles scattered throughout the Mediterranean world. Although Jesus himself never undertakes such a mission, his disciples will do precisely this, showing that the advance of the gospel beyond the borders of Israel is unwittingly announced by Christ's adversaries (Mt 28:18–20; Acts 1:8).

7:37 the great day: The seventh and final day of Tabernacles. **come to me and drink:** Jesus is the source of the spiritual "water" (4:10) that quenches our deepest "thirst" (6:35).

ᵇ Or *this man knows his letters.*

let him come to me and drink. ³⁸He who believes in me, as *q* the Scripture has said, 'Out of his heart shall flow rivers of living water.'" ³⁹Now this he said about the Spirit, which those who believed in him were to receive; for as yet the Spirit had not been given, because Jesus was not yet glorified.

Division among the People

40 When they heard these words, some of the people said, "This is really the prophet." ⁴¹Others said, "This is the Christ." But some said, "Is the Christ to come from Galilee? ⁴²Has not the Scripture said that the Christ is descended from David, and comes from Bethlehem, the village where David was?" ⁴³So there was a division among the people over him. ⁴⁴Some of them wanted to arrest him, but no one laid hands on him.

The Authorities and the Woman Caught in Adultery

45 The officers then went back to the chief priests and Pharisees, who said to them, "Why did you not bring him?" ⁴⁶The officers answered, "No man ever spoke like this man!" ⁴⁷The Pharisees answered them, "Are you led astray, you also?

⁴⁸Have any of the authorities or of the Pharisees believed in him? ⁴⁹But this crowd, who do not know the law, are accursed." ⁵⁰Nicode´mus, who had gone to him before, and who was one of them, said to them, ⁵¹"Does our law judge a man without first giving him a hearing and learning what he does?" ⁵²They replied, "Are you from Galilee too? Search and you will see that no prophet is to rise from Galilee." ⁵³They went each to his own house, 8 but Jesus went to the Mount of Olives. ²Early in the morning he came again to the temple; all the people came to him, and he sat down and taught them. ³The scribes and the Pharisees brought a woman who had been caught in adultery, and placing her in their midst ⁴they said to him, "Teacher, this woman has been caught in the act of adultery. ⁵Now in the law Moses commanded us to stone such. What do you say about her?" ⁶This they said to test him, that they might have some charge to bring against him. Jesus bent down and wrote with his finger on the ground. ⁷And as they continued to ask him, he stood up and said to them, "Let him who is without sin among you be the first to throw

---

7:38: Is 44:3; 55:1; 58:11.   7:39: Jn 20:22; 12:23.   7:40: Jn 1:21; Mt 21:11.   7:42: Mic 5:2; Mt 1:1; Lk 2:4.
7:44: Jn 7:30; 10:39.   7:46: Mt 7:28.   7:50: Jn 3:1; 19:39.   7:51: Deut 17:6; Ex 23:1.   7:52: 2 Kings 14:25.

The symbolic meaning of this is that Christ is the source of the Spirit poured out upon the world (7:39; 20:22). Jesus is probably alluding to the water-drawing ceremony of the feast, thus inviting us to think of him as the heavenly counterpart to the pool of Siloam. See notes on 7:2 and 9:7.

7:38 Out of his heart . . . living water: Not a verbatim reference to any one OT passage, but a summary or synthesis of at least three. • (1) In Num 20:10-13, Yahweh quenched Israel's thirst in the wilderness by making water gush forth from a rock. (2) In Ezek 47:1-12, the prophet sees water streaming forth from the Temple and bringing new life everywhere it flows. (3) In Zech 14:8, Jerusalem of the last days is depicted as a spring of living water that flows when the Lord becomes king over the earth and the nations come to celebrate the "feast of booths" (Tabernacles) year after year (Zech 14:9, 16). These traditions point forward to Jesus: he is the rock that slakes our thirst (1 Cor 10:4), the true temple that channels life to the world (2:21), and the Lord who reigns as king over the world (12:13; 18:36). See note on 19:34.

7:39 not yet glorified: i.e., through his Passion and Resurrection (12:23; 17:1). Only then will the Spirit be poured out through the risen humanity of Christ (20:22) (CCC 728, 1287).

7:40 the prophet: The awaited prophet like Moses from Deut 18:15-19. See note on 1:21.

7:41 the Christ: The awaited Messiah and king of Israel. See word study: *Christ* at Mk 14.

7:42 the Scripture: The Davidic lineage of the Messiah is mentioned in 2 Sam 7:12-14, Is 9:6-7, Jer 23:5, and Ezek 34:23-24, while his birthplace in Bethlehem is noted in Mic 5:2.

7:51 a hearing: Nicodemus pleads for due process and legal justice, only to be ridiculed by the Pharisees, just as the officers (7:47) and the people were (7:49).

7:53—8:11 Some ancient manuscripts of the Fourth Gospel omit this episode entirely. Other manuscripts place it elsewhere in John or even in the Gospel of Luke. According to the Council of Trent in the sixteenth century, the official canon of the Scriptures corresponds to everything included in the Latin Vulgate

edition (Sess. 4, Dec. 1). This translation includes the episode as canonical.

8:6 to test him: The Pharisees are not seeking legal advice from Jesus. Their question in 8:5 is a trap designed to incriminate or discredit him. (1) If Jesus *authorizes* the stoning, the Pharisees will report him to the Romans for criminal wrongdoing, for the Jews were not permitted to administer capital punishment under Roman rule (18:31). (2) If Jesus *forbids* the stoning, the Pharisees will discredit him as a false messiah who contradicts Moses, for the Torah classifies adultery as a capital crime (Lev 20:10; Deut 22:22).

8:7 Let him who is without sin: Many popular interpretations of this verse are unworkable because they lead Jesus straight into the trap set by the Pharisees in 8:4-5. (1) Some argue that Jesus is overturning the death penalty for adultery prescribed in the Torah. This could not have been so because the Pharisees would have immediately discredited him for contradicting Moses. In fact, Jesus is not addressing the status or legality of the death penalty at all; he is simply dodging the Pharisees' trap. (2) Others argue that Jesus permits the adulteress to walk free because no witnesses are present to testify against her. This could not have been so, first, because it wrongly implies that Jesus would have been caught off guard if the witnesses who caught the adulteress in the act did come forward and, second, because it wrongly implies that Jesus would then have authorized the stoning. (3) Others argue that Jesus brings the examination to a halt because the woman's partner is absent and so the process of incrimination cannot proceed. This could not have been so, first, because of a clear precedent in the OT where Susanna is falsely condemned for adultery without first establishing who and where her partner was (Dan 13:34-41) and, second, because it wrongly implies that Jesus would have authorized the stoning if the woman's partner had eventually been found. Against these views, it must be stressed that Jesus eludes the trap entirely—he neither authorizes the stoning (incriminating himself) nor contradicts Moses (compromising his teaching). The genius of his response is that it turns the tables on the Pharisees and forces them into their own trap. Although the Pharisees probably considered themselves sinless (like Saul, Phil 3:5-6), and thus qualified to

---

q Or *let him come to me, and let him who believes in me drink. As.*

a stone at her." ⁸And once more he bent down and wrote with his finger on the ground. ⁹But when they heard it, they went away, one by one, beginning with the eldest, and Jesus was left alone with the woman standing before him. ¹⁰Jesus looked up and said to her, "Woman, where are they? Has no one condemned you?" ¹¹She said, "No one, Lord." And Jesus said, "Neither do I condemn you; go, and do not sin again."ʳ

Jesus and the Light of the World

12 Again Jesus spoke to them, saying, "I am the light of the world; he who follows me will not walk in darkness, but will have the light of life." ¹³The Pharisees then said to him, "You are bearing witness to yourself; your testimony is not true." ¹⁴Jesus answered, "Even if I do bear witness to myself, my testimony is true, for I know where I have come from and where I am going, but you do not know where I come from or where I am going. ¹⁵You judge according to the flesh, I judge no one. ¹⁶Yet even if I do judge, my judgment is true, for it is not I alone that judge, but I and heˢ who sent me. ¹⁷In your law it is written that the testimony of two men is true; ¹⁸I bear witness to myself, and the Father who sent me bears witness to me." ¹⁹They said to him therefore, "Where is your Father?" Jesus answered, "You know neither me nor my Father; if you knew me, you would know my Father also." ²⁰These words he spoke in the treasury, as he taught in the temple; but no one arrested him, because his hour had not yet come.

Jesus Alludes to His Death

21 Again he said to them, "I go away, and you will seek me and die in your sin; where I am going, you cannot come." ²²Then said the Jews, "Will he kill himself, since he says, 'Where I am going, you cannot come'?" ²³He said to them, "You are from below, I am from above; you are of this world, I am not of this world. ²⁴I told you that you would die in your sins, for you will die in your sins unless you believe that I am he." ²⁵They said to him, "Who are you?" Jesus said to them, "Even what I have told you from the beginning.ᵗ ²⁶I have much to say about you and much to judge; but he who sent me is true, and I declare to the world what I have heard from him." ²⁷They did not understand that he spoke to them of the Father. ²⁸So Jesus said, "When you have lifted up the Son of man, then you will know that I am he, and that I do nothing on my own authority but speak thus as the Father taught me. ²⁹And he who sent me is with me; he has not left me alone, for I always do what is pleasing to him." ³⁰As he spoke thus, many believed in him.

True Disciples of Jesus

31 Jesus then said to the Jews who had believed in him, "If you continue in my word, you are truly my disciples, ³²and you will know the truth, and

---

8:12: Jn 9:5; 12:35; 1:4.   8:13–18: Jn 5:31–39.   8:15: Jn 7:24; 3:17.   8:16: Jn 5:30.   8:17: Deut 19:15; Mt 18:16.
8:19: Jn 14:7.   8:20: Mk 12:41; Jn 7:30.   8:21–22: Jn 7:33–36.   8:23: Jn 3:31; 17:14; 1 Jn 4:5.
8:24: Jn 8:28; 4:26; 13:19; Mk 13:6.   8:28: Jn 3:14; 12:32.   8:30: Jn 7:31; 10:42; 11:45.   8:31: Jn 15:7; 2 Jn 9.
8:32: 2 Cor 3:17; Gal 5:1.

---

administer the stoning, they realize that executing the adulteress will bring Rome's reprisal on *them* instead of Jesus, who is not truly authorizing the stoning because he does not truly think the Pharisees are without sin (9:40–41). On the other hand, by restraining themselves and walking away, the Pharisees are made to look like *sinners* and *compromisers* in the eyes of the crowd.

8:8 wrote . . . on the ground: What Jesus inscribes in the dirt is unknown but probably symbolic. ● The gesture may recall Jer 17:13, a warning that those who forsake the Lord "shall be written in the earth" because they have rejected the "fountain of living water". The Pharisees fall into this category for rejecting Jesus, who has just been identified as the source of "living water" (7:38). ● *Morally* (St. Bede, *Hom. in Evan.*), Christ, who twice bends down to write on the ground, teaches us to bend low in humility to examine ourselves both before and after addressing the faults of our neighbor. If his example becomes our practice, we will avoid as he did the extremes of being unjust and unmerciful toward others.

8:9 the eldest: i.e., the wisest, who were the first to detect the brilliance of Jesus' reply (8:7).

8:11 do not sin again: Jesus neither condemns the woman nor condones her sins. He rather forgives her past and challenges her to live a life of purity in the future (see also 5:14).

8:12 the light of the world: Christ enlightens the world with truth as the golden candelabras illuminated the Temple courts with fire during the feast of Tabernacles. The location of Jesus as he delivers these words supports this symbolism: he is standing in the "treasury" adjacent to the Court of Women (8:20), precisely where the lamp-lighting ceremony was recently conducted. See note on 7:2. ● Several OT themes prepared the way for Jesus, the "true light" (1:9). (1) Ex 13:21 describes how Yahweh, enthroned in a pillar of fire, enlightened the way for Israel to travel through the wilderness toward the Promised Land. (2) Ps 119:105 describes the Law of the Lord as a light for our path. (3) Is 42:6 and 49:6 call Israel to be a light to the nations.

8:15 according to the flesh: i.e., on the basis of limited human reason. See note on 6:63.

8:17 it is written: Deut 17:6 and 19:15 require two or three witnesses to establish credible legal testimony in court.

8:20 his hour: See topical essay: *The "Hour" of Jesus* at Jn 4.

8:23 from below: Not from hell but from the earth. Jesus comes from heaven above (3:31).

8:24 you will die: An assurance not simply of bodily death, which is the fate of everyone, but of spiritual death, which irrevocably separates sinners from God for all eternity. **I am:** Recalls the name of Yahweh revealed to Moses at the burning bush. See note on 6:20. ● Jesus stresses in this context the importance of *believing* (8:24) and *knowing* (8:28) that he is the great "I AM". This evokes Is 43:10–11, where witnesses from Israel come to "know" and "believe" that the Lord is truly the God of their forefathers, the sovereign "I AM".

8:28 lifted up the Son: i.e., in his Passion, Resurrection, and Ascension. See note on 12:32.

8:32 truth will make you free: Jesus embodies divine truth (14:6) and has come to bear witness to the truth (18:37). Acceptance of him liberates us from the slavery of sin, ignorance, and deception (8:12; CCC 2466).

ʳ Some ancient authorities insert 7:53–8:11 either at the end of this gospel or after Luke 21:38, with variations of the text. Others omit it altogether.
ˢ Other ancient authorities read *the Father.*
ᵗ Or *Why do I talk to you at all?*

the truth will make you free." [33]They answered him, "We are descendants of Abraham, and have never been in bondage to any one. How is it that you say, 'You will be made free'?"

[34] Jesus answered them, "Truly, truly, I say to you, every one who commits sin is a slave to sin. [35]The slave does not continue in the house for ever; the son continues for ever. [36]So if the Son makes you free, you will be free indeed. [37]I know that you are descendants of Abraham; yet you seek to kill me, because my word finds no place in you. [38]I speak of what I have seen with my Father, and you do what you have heard from your father."

Jesus and Abraham

[39] They answered him, "Abraham is our father." Jesus said to them, "If you were Abraham's children, you would do what Abraham did, [40]but now you seek to kill me, a man who has told you the truth which I heard from God; this is not what Abraham did. [41]You do the works of your father." They said to him, "We were not born of fornication; we have one Father, even God." [42]Jesus said to them, "If God were your Father, you would love me, for I proceeded and came forth from God; I came not of my own accord, but he sent me. [43]Why do you not understand what I say? It is because you cannot bear to hear my word. [44]You are of your father the devil, and your will is to do your father's desires. He was a murderer from the beginning,

and has nothing to do with the truth, because there is no truth in him. When he lies, he speaks according to his own nature, for he is a liar and the father of lies. [45]But, because I tell the truth, you do not believe me. [46]Which of you convicts me of sin? If I tell the truth, why do you not believe me? [47]He who is of God hears the words of God; the reason why you do not hear them is that you are not of God."

[48] The Jews answered him, "Are we not right in saying that you are a Samaritan and have a demon?" [49]Jesus answered, "I have not a demon; but I honor my Father, and you dishonor me. [50]Yet I do not seek my own glory; there is One who seeks it and he will be the judge. [51]Truly, truly, I say to you, if any one keeps my word, he will never see death." [52]The Jews said to him, "Now we know that you have a demon. Abraham died, as did the prophets; and you say, 'If any one keeps my word, he will never taste death.' [53]Are you greater than our father Abraham, who died? And the prophets died! Who do you claim to be?" [54]Jesus answered, "If I glorify myself, my glory is nothing; it is my Father who glorifies me, of whom you say that he is your God. [55]But you have not known him; I know him. If I said, I do not know him, I should be a liar like you; but I do know him and I keep his word. [56]Your father Abraham rejoiced that he was to see my day; he saw it and was glad." [57]The Jews then said to him, "You are not yet fifty years old, and have

---

8:33: Mt 3:9; Gal 3:7.   **8:34:** Rom 6:16; 2 Pet 2:19.   **8:35:** Gen 21:10; Gal 4:30.   **8:41:** Deut 32:6; Is 63:16; 64:8.
8:42: Jn 13:3; 16:28.   **8:44:** 1 Jn 3:8, 15; Gen 3:4; 1 Jn 2:4; Mt 12:34.   **8:46:** 1 Jn 3:5; Jn 18:37.   **8:48:** Jn 7:20; 10:20; 4:9.
8:53: Jn 4:12.   **8:56:** Mt 13:17; Heb 11:13.   **8:57:** Jn 2:20.

8:33–47 The exchange between Jesus and the Jewish authorities turns around the question of family identity. Jesus is the Son of his heavenly Father, who extends the gift of sonship to those who accept his word (1:12; 8:36). Those claiming that Abraham is their father are denied the status of Abrahamic sonship, not because they have no genealogical ties to the patriarch, but because they do not imitate his faith (8:39–40). They are rather sons of Satan, for the character traits of their father, the devil, are manifest in them as they reject the word of Jesus and seek to kill him (8:40, 44).

8:33 never been in bondage: An almost ridiculous response. Throughout biblical history, Israel had been enslaved by the Egyptians, subjugated by the Philistines, Assyrians, Babylonians, and Persians, and was now in the grip of Imperial Rome. These forms of political domination were merely symptoms of Israel's slavery to sin.

8:34 slave to sin: Man is powerless to break free from the devil and the bondage of his own weaknesses. This predicament entangles everyone, Israelites and Gentiles alike (Rom 3:9). Christ alone can liberate slaves of the devil and make them sons of the Father (Gal 4:3–7) (CCC 549, 1741).

8:35 The slave . . . the son: Jesus alludes to the story of Abraham's two sons, Ishmael and Isaac, to demonstrate that genealogical descent from the patriarch does not guarantee the blessing of divine sonship in the New Covenant. • Ishmael was born to Abraham by a slave woman, Hagar (Gen 16:15), while Isaac was born to Abraham by his lawful wife, Sarah (Gen 21:3). Though both were the natural sons of Abraham, Ishmael was later expelled from Abraham's family, disinherited, and excluded from the blessings of the covenant (Gen 17:19–21; 21:10–14). Jesus applies this narrative to the sons of Abraham in his own day: Unless they accept him in faith and become sons of God (1:12), they will follow the way of

Ishmael, being driven out from the house of Abraham and cut off from the blessings promised to his descendants (Gal 4:21–31).

8:44 your father the devil: A bold indictment of Israel's leadership. They are sons neither of Abraham (8:40) nor of God the Father (8:42), but are the offspring of a murderer, liar, and deceiver (CCC 391, 2482).

8:46 convicts me of sin?: Jesus is completely unstained by sin, as is his conscience (Heb 4:15; 1 Pet 2:22; CCC 578).

8:48 a Samaritan: An insult implying that Jesus was born of mixed racial parentage and followed a deviant form of religion. See note on 4:7–42. **have a demon:** A common charge leveled at Jesus (7:20; 10:20; Mt 9:34; 12:24). • *Morally* (St. Gregory the Great, *Homily* 18), Jesus sets the example of perfect composure in the face of insults, since he denied the charge of being a demoniac but did not counter it with an abusive response. If Jesus did not avenge himself, then neither should we return injury for injury when reviled by our neighbor.

8:51 never see death: Not that Jesus exempts believers from the experience of bodily death, but that he saves their souls from spiritual death by the gift of eternal life (Rom 6:23).

8:56 to see my day: Probably a reference to the events in Gen 22:1–18. • (1) When Abraham nearly sacrifices Isaac as a holocaust, only to receive him back alive, the patriarch witnessed a *preview* of the Father surrendering his Son to death and receiving him back in the Resurrection (Heb 11:17–19). (2) In response to this act of faith, Yahweh rewarded Abraham with a sworn covenant *promise* that one of his descendants would arise to bless all nations (Gen 22:16–18). This oath is fulfilled in the dying and rising of Jesus, who sends blessings to every nation (Mt 28:18–20; Gal 3:14; CCC 706).

8:57 not yet fifty years old: Jesus is only in his early thirties (Lk 3:23).

you seen Abraham?" [u] [58]Jesus said to them, "Truly, truly, I say to you, before Abraham was, I am." [59]So they took up stones to throw at him; but Jesus hid himself, and went out of the temple.

Healing of the Blind Man

9 As he passed by, he saw a man blind from his birth. [2]And his disciples asked him, "Rabbi, who sinned, this man or his parents, that he was born blind?" [3]Jesus answered, "It was not that this man sinned, or his parents, but that the works of God might be made manifest in him. [4]We must work the works of him who sent me, while it is day; night comes, when no one can work. [5]As long as I am in the world, I am the light of the world." [6]As he said this, he spat on the ground and made clay of the spittle and anointed the man's eyes with the clay, [7]saying to him, "Go, wash in the pool of Silo'am" (which means Sent). So he went and washed and came back seeing. [8]The neighbors and those who had seen him before as a beggar, said, "Is not this the man who used to sit and beg?" [9]Some said, "It is he"; others said, "No, but he is like him." He said, "I am the man." [10]They said to him, "Then how were your eyes opened?" [11]He answered, "The man called Jesus made clay and anointed my eyes and said to me, 'Go to Silo'am and wash'; so I went and washed and received my sight." [12]They said to him, "Where is he?" He said, "I do not know."

The Pharisees Investigate the Healing

13 They brought to the Pharisees the man who had formerly been blind. [14]Now it was a sabbath day when Jesus made the clay and opened his eyes. [15]The Pharisees again asked him how he had received his sight. And he said to them, "He put clay on my eyes, and I washed, and I see." [16]Some of the Pharisees said, "This man is not from God, for he does not keep the sabbath." But others said, "How can a man who is a sinner do such signs?" There was a division among them. [17]So they again said to the blind man, "What do you say about him, since he has opened your eyes?" He said, "He is a prophet."

18 The Jews did not believe that he had been blind and had received his sight, until they called the parents of the man who had received his sight, [19]and asked them, "Is this your son, who you say was born blind? How then does he now see?" [20]His parents answered, "We know that this is our son, and that he was born blind; [21]but how he now sees we do not know, nor do we know who opened his eyes. Ask him; he is of age, he will speak for himself." [22]His parents said this because they feared the Jews, for the Jews had already agreed that if any one should confess him to be Christ, he was to be put out of the synagogue. [23]Therefore his parents said, "He is of age, ask him."

24 So for the second time they called the man who had been blind, and said to him, "Give God the praise; we know that this man is a sinner." [25]He answered, "Whether he is a sinner, I do not know; one thing I know, that though I was blind, now I see." [26]They said to him, "What did he do to you?

8:58: Jn 1:1; 17:5, 24.   **8:59:** Jn 10:31; 11:8.   **9:2:** Lk 13:2; Acts 28:4; Ezek 18:20; Ex 20:5.   **9:3:** Jn 11:4.   **9:4:** Jn 11:9; 12:35.   **9:5:** Jn 1:4; 8:12; 12:46.   **9:6:** Mk 7:33; 8:23.   **9:7:** Lk 13:4.   **9:16:** Mt 12:2; Jn 5:9; 7:43; 10:19.   **9:22:** Jn 7:13; 12:42; Lk 6:22.

8:58 before Abraham was, I am: Jesus takes for himself the divine name of Yahweh, "I AM" (Ex 3:14). He thus claims to be one with God (10:30), whose life in eternity has neither beginning nor end. The Pharisees hear this claim loud and clear and, thinking it outrageous, stand ready to stone him for blasphemy (8:59; Lev 24:16) (CCC 590). See notes on 1:1 and 6:20.

9:2 Rabbi, who sinned . . . ?: Sickness was thought to be a direct consequence of sin (Job 31:3; Ps 107:17). Responsibility for physical ailments was imputed either to one's parents (Tob 3:3) or to the earliest period of one's life, since certain rabbis taught that infants could sin before birth (9:34). Jesus does not deny the *principle* that sickness is brought on by sin, but that a *personal* link can be established in every case.

9:3 the works of God: The man's blindness was part of the providential plan of God (11:4). Giving physical sight to the blind is a sign that Jesus gives us spiritual sight to see earth in light of heaven, time in light of eternity, and our lives in light of our destiny.

9:5 I am the light: Jesus is the source of all truth, faith, and life (1:9; 14:6; 18:37). See note on 8:12.

9:6 made clay of the spittle: The use of common materials to serve a holy purpose anticipates Jesus' institution of the seven sacraments. See note on Mk 6:56.

9:7 Go, wash: Recalls the miracle of Elisha in 2 Kings 5:10–14. ● Elisha commanded Naaman the Syrian to "go and wash" in the Jordan River to be restored to health. **the pool of Siloam:** A rock-hewn reservoir in the southern district of ancient Jerusalem. The pool was built by King Hezekiah

to serve as a water supply for the city (2 Kings 20:20; 2 Chron 32:30). The editorial comment that Siloam means **Sent** suggests that the pool is a symbol of Jesus, the source of living water (4:10) and the One sent by his Father (9:4; 12:44). Its contents are symbolic of the Spirit, who is the living water poured out by Christ (7:38–39) and the One who is sent by the Father and the Son (14:26; 15:26). ● The miracle anticipates the administration of Baptism, where catechumens are *washed* (9:7) in water, *anointed* (9:6) with oil, and *enlightened* with grace and truth (9:5; Eph 1:18; Heb 6:4; CCC 1216).

9:11 The man called Jesus: The perception of Jesus deepens as the story unfolds: here he is a "man"; by verse 9:17 he is a "prophet"; by 9:33 he is "from God"; and by 9:38 he is "Lord" worthy of worship. The narrative challenges our minds to make the same conclusion and our hearts to make the same response.

9:14 sabbath day: Instead of rejoicing with the man cured of blindness, the Pharisees haggle over the supposed illegality of the miracle on the sacred day of rest. They are missing the fact that Jesus fulfills the true intent of the Sabbath by offering the man "rest" after long years of being handicapped (CCC 2173).

9:19 Is this your son . . . ?: The testimony of the man's parents would be the most credible of all since they would have known him from birth (9:20).

9:22 put out of the synagogue: i.e., excommunicated from the fellowship and worship of the Jews (Ezra 10:8). This was a frightful prospect for many Jewish Christians in the early Church (12:42; 16:2).

9:24 Give God the praise: An oath formula that binds a witness to speak the truth (Josh 7:19).

[u] Other ancient authorities read *has Abraham seen you?*

How did he open your eyes?" ²⁷He answered them, "I have told you already, and you would not listen. Why do you want to hear it again? Do you too want to become his disciples?" ²⁸And they reviled him, saying, "You are his disciple, but we are disciples of Moses. ²⁹We know that God has spoken to Moses, but as for this man, we do not know where he comes from." ³⁰The man answered, "Why, this is a marvel! You do not know where he comes from, and yet he opened my eyes. ³¹We know that God does not listen to sinners, but if any one is a worshiper of God and does his will, God listens to him. ³²Never since the world began has it been heard that any one opened the eyes of a man born blind. ³³If this man were not from God, he could do nothing." ³⁴They answered him, "You were born in utter sin, and would you teach us?" And they cast him out.

Spiritual Blindness

35 Jesus heard that they had cast him out, and having found him he said, "Do you believe in the Son of man?" ᵛ ³⁶He answered, "And who is he, sir, that I may believe in him?" ³⁷Jesus said to him, "You have seen him, and it is he who speaks to you." ³⁸He said, "Lord, I believe"; and he worshiped him. ³⁹Jesus said, "For judgment I came into this world, that those who do not see may see, and that those who see may become blind." ⁴⁰Some of the Pharisees near him heard this, and they said to him, "Are we also blind?" ⁴¹Jesus said to them, "If you were blind, you would have no guilt; but now that you say, 'We see,' your guilt remains.

Jesus the Good Shepherd

10 "Truly, truly, I say to you, he who does not enter the sheepfold by the door but climbs in by another way, that man is a thief and a robber; ²but he who enters by the door is the shepherd of the sheep. ³To him the gatekeeper opens; the sheep hear his voice, and he calls his own sheep by name and leads them out. ⁴When he has brought out all his own, he goes before them, and the sheep follow him, for they know his voice. ⁵A stranger they will not follow, but they will flee from him, for they do not know the voice of strangers." ⁶This figure Jesus used with them, but they did not understand what he was saying to them.

7 So Jesus again said to them, "Truly, truly, I say to you, I am the door of the sheep. ⁸All who came before me are thieves and robbers; but the sheep did not heed them. ⁹I am the door; if any one enters by me, he will be saved, and will go in and out and find pasture. ¹⁰The thief comes only to steal and kill and destroy; I came that they may have life, and have it abundantly. ¹¹I am the good shepherd. The good shepherd lays down his life for the sheep. ¹²He who is a hireling and not a shepherd, whose own the sheep are not, sees the wolf coming and leaves the sheep and flees; and the wolf snatches them and scatters them. ¹³He flees because he is a hireling and cares nothing for the sheep. ¹⁴I am the good shepherd; I know my own and my own know me, ¹⁵as the Father knows me and I know the Father; and I lay down my life for the sheep. ¹⁶And I have other sheep, that are not of this fold; I must

---

9:28: Jn 5:45.   **9:38:** Mt 28:9.   **9:39:** Jn 5:27; 3:19; Mt 15:14.   **9:41:** Jn 15:22.   **10:2:** Mk 6:34.   **10:6:** Jn 16:25.
10:8: Jer 23:1; Ezek 34:2.   **10:11:** Is 40:11; Ezek 34:11–16; Heb 13:20; 1 Pet 5:4; Rev 7:17; 1 Jn 3:16; Jn 15:13.   **10:15:** Mt 11:27.
10:16: Is 56:8; Jn 11:52; 17:20; Eph 2:13–18; 1 Pet 2:25.

9:32 Never . . . opened the eyes: Even Tobit, whose eyesight was temporarily lost and later restored, was not blind from birth (Tob 2:9–10; 11:7–15; 14:1–2).

9:33 he could do nothing: Mirrors the logic of Nicodemus in 3:2.

9:35 the Son of man: The heavenly figure from Dan 7:13. See topical essay: *Jesus, the Son of Man* at Lk 17.

9:39 may see . . . become blind: To the humble and childlike, Jesus reveals the Father and his will, but to the wise and understanding, he withholds the light necessary to see the truth (Mt 11:25–27; 13:13–16). The Pharisees fall in the latter category because, while they claim to see clearly, they are blind to their deepest spiritual needs (9:41).

10:1 the sheepfold: Probably a stone wall enclosure with a single entryway, used to protect flocks at night from thieves and predators. Only the shepherd would be recognized and admitted by the designated gatekeeper (10:3). The whole illustration gives a realistic portrayal of pastoral conditions in ancient Palestine (10:1–16).

10:3 calls . . . by name: A mark of intimacy and familiarity (Is 43:1; 49:1). **leads them out:** To graze and find pasture (10:9). The sheep are disciples who hear the voice of Jesus and follow him wherever he goes. ● The expression "to lead out" recalls how Joshua was appointed to lead Israel out of the wilderness (Num 27:17) and how Yahweh promised to recover the lost sheep of Israel by leading them out of their exile among the nations (Ezek 34:13). See note on 10:11.

10:6 they did not understand: The Pharisees, who are blind to the spiritual dimension of Jesus' teaching (9:39–41).

10:8 All who came before: Refers to the shepherds of Israel, many of whom were denounced by the prophets as worthless and evil (Jer 23:1–3; Ezek 34:1–10; Zech 11:17). The Pharisees are their spiritual descendants (Mt 23:29–36).

10:10 have life: Divine life. See note on 3:16.

10:11 I am the good shepherd: Jesus leads his flock away from dangers and into safe pastures. He is so committed to the welfare of each one of his sheep that he is willing to die for them (10:17–18; CCC 609). ● Although Yahweh was the divine shepherd of Israel (Ps 23:1), he exercised his rule through earthly shepherds like Joshua and David (Num 27:16–18; 2 Sam 5:2). A similar arrangement was expected for the last days, when the Lord would shepherd the flock of his people through the Davidic Messiah (Ezek 34:11–24). Note that David himself was a good shepherd, who, before his kingship over Israel, risked his life to deliver his flock from predators that tried to kill them (1 Sam 17:34–36).

10:12 the wolf: A traditional symbol of spiritual enemies (Mt 7:15; 10:16; Acts 20:29).

10:16 other sheep: A reference to the Gentiles, who are gathered into the Messiah's flock alongside the restored sheep of Israel (11:52). **one flock, one shepherd:** Jesus Christ is the supreme Shepherd over the one universal Church (Heb 13:20). The spiritual authority of other shepherds like Peter and the apostles is derived entirely from Christ, who gives disciples a share in his saving mission to different degrees (21:15–17; CCC 553, 754). ● The Apostles' Creed delineates the four marks of the Church as "one, holy, catholic, and apostolic". The

---

ᵛ Other ancient authorities read *the Son of God.*

bring them also, and they will heed my voice. So there shall be one flock, one shepherd. ¹⁷For this reason the Father loves me, because I lay down my life, that I may take it again. ¹⁸No one takes it from me, but I lay it down of my own accord. I have power to lay it down, and I have power to take it again; this charge I have received from my Father."

19 There was again a division among the Jews because of these words. ²⁰Many of them said, "He has a demon, and he is mad; why listen to him?" ²¹Others said, "These are not the sayings of one who has a demon. Can a demon open the eyes of the blind?"

Jesus Is Rejected by the Jews

22 It was the feast of the Dedication at Jerusalem; ²³it was winter, and Jesus was walking in the temple, in the portico of Solomon. ²⁴So the Jews gathered round him and said to him, "How long will you keep us in suspense? If you are the Christ, tell us plainly." ²⁵Jesus answered them, "I told you, and you do not believe. The works that I do in my Father's name, they bear witness to me; ²⁶but you do not believe, because you do not belong to my sheep. ²⁷My sheep hear my voice, and I know them, and they follow me; ²⁸and I give them eternal life, and they shall never perish, and no one shall snatch them out of my hand. ²⁹My Father, who has given

them to me,ʷ is greater than all, and no one is able to snatch them out of the Father's hand. ³⁰I and the Father are one."

31 The Jews took up stones again to stone him. ³²Jesus answered them, "I have shown you many good works from the Father; for which of these do you stone me?" ³³The Jews answered him, "We stone you for no good work but for blasphemy; because you, being a man, make yourself God." ³⁴Jesus answered them, "Is it not written in your law, 'I said, you are gods'? ³⁵If he called them gods to whom the word of God came (and Scripture cannot be nullified), ³⁶do you say of him whom the Father consecrated and sent into the world, 'You are blaspheming,' because I said, 'I am the Son of God'? ³⁷If I am not doing the works of my Father, then do not believe me; ³⁸but if I do them, even though you do not believe me, believe the works, that you may know and understand that the Father is in me and I am in the Father." ³⁹Again they tried to arrest him, but he escaped from their hands.

40 He went away again across the Jordan to the place where John at first baptized, and there he remained. ⁴¹And many came to him; and they said, "John did no sign, but everything that John said about this man was true." ⁴²And many believed in him there.

10:18: Jn 14:31; 15:10; Phil 2:8; Heb 5:8. **10:19:** Jn 7:43; 9:16. **10:20:** Jn 7:20; 8:48; Mt 11:18. **10:21:** Jn 9:32; Ex 4:11. **10:23:** Acts 3:11; 5:12. **10:25:** Jn 5:36; 10:38. **10:26:** Jn 8:47. **10:28:** Jn 17:2; 1 Jn 2:25. **10:30:** Jn 17:21. **10:31:** Jn 8:59; 11:8. **10:33:** Lev 24:16; Mk 14:64. **10:34:** Jn 8:17; Ps 82:6. **10:39:** Jn 7:30; 8:59; Lk 4:30. **10:40:** Jn 1:28. **10:42:** Jn 7:31; 11:45.

---

first mark, oneness, means that the Church is unified in her faith, worship, and leadership and receives her life from the one true God (17:11; Eph 4:4–6) (CCC 813–22).

10:17 lay down my life . . . take it again: Only God himself, who has absolute power over life and death, could make such a claim and hope to fulfill it (2:19; CCC 609).

10:22 feast of the Dedication: Also called "Hanukkah". It is an eight-day winter festival that celebrates Israel's deliverance from Syrian oppression as well as Judas Maccabeus' cleansing and rededication of the Jerusalem Temple in 164 B.C. (1 Mac 4:36–59; 2 Mac 10:1–8). **the portico of Solomon:** Colonnade walkways surrounded the outer perimeter of the Temple. The section running along the eastern side was named after King Solomon (Acts 3:11).

10:24 tell us plainly: The antagonism between Jesus and his enemies kept him from broadcasting his messianic mission openly. See note on Mk 1:44.

📖 **10:28 out of my hand:** The protection that Jesus provides for his sheep is equivalent to the Father's divine protection (10:29). • This means, from the perspective of the OT, that Christ wields the sovereign power of Yahweh to shield the righteous from the threats of their enemies (Deut 32:39; Wis 3:1; Is 43:13).

10:30 I and the Father are one: The Father and the Son are united in the loving embrace of the Spirit. We cannot, therefore, divide the essential unity of the Trinity when we distinguish between the three Divine Persons. See note on 1:1 and 5:18.

📖 **10:34 your law:** Sometimes this expression refers to the OT in general and not just to the Pentateuch (12:34; 15:25; 1 Cor 14:34). **I said, you are gods:** A citation from Ps 82:6. • The psalm is a prayer for Yahweh to punish the cor-

rupt shepherds of Israel. These leaders, who are charged with teaching and enforcing divine Law, are called "gods" by the Psalmist because of the divine authority they wield over the people. The abuse of this power makes their corruption all the more insidious. Jesus reasons that if sinful authorities are given a divine title because of their duties, how much more is he entitled to it who is guiltless and who speaks the words of God (8:45–47).

10:35 Scripture cannot be nullified: Three implications can be drawn from this statement. (1) Scripture cannot be set aside, since its teaching is as trustworthy and true as God himself (17:17). (2) The OT, represented in this context by a psalm, has permanent authority even under the New Covenant (Mt 5:17). (3) The authority of Scripture extends even to individual words, as in this context where Jesus' whole argument rests on the import of a single word ("gods") from Ps 82:6.

📖 **10:36 consecrated:** The Greek means to be "sanctified" or "set apart as holy". Christ is set apart by the Father to consecrate the world in truth (17:19). • Jesus' words resonate against the background of the Feast of the Dedication, which celebrates the *consecration* of the Second Temple by the Maccabees (1 Mac 4:48), just as its predecessors, the wilderness Tabernacle (Num 7:1) and the Solomonic Temple, had been consecrated (1 Kings 9:3). These sanctuaries of old are replaced by the new and consecrated temple of Jesus' body (2:20–21).

10:38 believe the works: The miracles of Jesus are meant to authenticate his mission in the eyes of Israel (5:36; 14:11) and to corroborate his claims to divinity (5:18; 10:33). The Jews knew that only God, who has absolute power over creation, can suspend the laws of nature in a miraculous way (3:2; 9:33) (CCC 548).

10:40 where John . . . baptized: An unknown location near Bethany, east of the Jordan River (1:28).

ʷ Other ancient authorities read *What my Father has given to me.*

The Death of Lazarus

11 Now a certain man was ill, Laz´arus of Bethany, the village of Mary and her sister Martha. ²It was Mary who anointed the Lord with ointment and wiped his feet with her hair, whose brother Laz´arus was ill. ³So the sisters sent to him, saying, "Lord, he whom you love is ill." ⁴But when Jesus heard it he said, "This illness is not unto death; it is for the glory of God, so that the Son of God may be glorified by means of it."

5 Now Jesus loved Martha and her sister and Laz´arus. ⁶So when he heard that he was ill, he stayed two days longer in the place where he was. ⁷Then after this he said to the disciples, "Let us go into Judea again." ⁸The disciples said to him, "Rabbi, the Jews were but now seeking to stone you, and are you going there again?" ⁹Jesus answered, "Are there not twelve hours in the day? If any one walks in the day, he does not stumble, because he sees the light of this world. ¹⁰But if any one walks in the night, he stumbles, because the light is not in him." ¹¹Thus he spoke, and then he said to them, "Our friend Laz´arus has fallen asleep, but I go to awake him out of sleep." ¹²The disciples said to him, "Lord, if he has fallen asleep, he will recover." ¹³Now Jesus had spoken of his death, but they thought that he meant taking rest in sleep. ¹⁴Then Jesus told them plainly, "Laz´arus is dead; ¹⁵and for your sake I am glad that I was not there, so that you may believe. But let us go to him." ¹⁶Thomas, called the Twin, said to his fellow disciples, "Let us also go, that we may die with him."

Jesus the Resurrection and the Life

17 Now when Jesus came, he found that Laz´arus *x* had already been in the tomb four days. ¹⁸Bethany was near Jerusalem, about two miles *y* off, ¹⁹and many of the Jews had come to Martha and Mary to console them concerning their brother. ²⁰When Martha heard that Jesus was coming, she went and met him, while Mary sat in the house. ²¹Martha said to Jesus, "Lord, if you had been here, my brother would not have died. ²²And even now I know that whatever you ask from God, God will give you." ²³Jesus said to her, "Your brother will rise again." ²⁴Martha said to him, "I know that he will rise again in the resurrection at the last day." ²⁵Jesus said to her, "I am the resurrection and the life; *z* he who believes in me, though he die, yet shall he live, ²⁶and whoever lives and believes in me shall never die. Do you believe this?" ²⁷She said to him, "Yes, Lord; I believe that you are the Christ, the Son of God, he who is coming into the world."

11:1: Mk 11:1; Lk 10:38.   **11:2:** Jn 12:3; Lk 7:38; Mk 14:3.   **11:4:** Jn 9:3.   **11:8:** Jn 8:59; 10:31.
11:9: Jn 9:4; 12:35; Lk 13:33.   **11:11:** Mk 5:39; Acts 7:60.   **11:16:** Mt 10:3; Jn 20:24–28.   **11:19:** Job 2:11.
11:24: Dan 12:2; Jn 5:28; Acts 24:15.   **11:25:** Jn 1:4; 5:26; Rev 1:18.   **11:26:** Jn 6:47; 8:51.   **11:27:** Mt 16:16.

11:1–44 The raising of Lazarus is the sixth of seven "signs" that Jesus performs in John (12:18), giving emphatic support to his claim to give "life" (5:25–29; 6:40). There is a dark side to the episode as well, as it provokes Jewish opposition that will precipitate Jesus' death (11:45–53). Similar miracles are recorded in the Synoptic Gospels, such as the raising of Jairus' daughter (Mk 5:21–43) and the raising of the widow's son from Nain (Lk 7:11–17) (CCC 994). See word study: *Signs* at Jn 2. ● Precedent for raising the dead was set by the prophets Elijah (1 Kings 17:17–24) and Elisha (2 Kings 4:32–37).

11:1 Lazarus: A beloved friend of Jesus (11:5). **Bethany:** A small village about two miles east of Jerusalem (11:18). **Mary . . . Martha:** Possibly the friends of Jesus mentioned in Lk 10:38–42. The personalities of these two women in John, with Martha as the busy hostess (12:2) and Mary giving her attention to Jesus (12:3), make this identification probable.

11:2 Mary who anointed the Lord: Anticipates the following episode in 12:1–8.

11:4 not unto death: Lazarus will in fact die (11:14). But this will not be his ultimate fate because Jesus will raise him to new life, affording an opportunity for others to glorify God by means of the miracle (9:3).

11:6 two days longer: The delay of Jesus proves fatal for Lazarus. This period of waiting is not a mistake or miscalculation, but part of his plan to generate faith in the disciples (11:15, 42). Raising the dead to new life will have a more profound effect on them than raising the sick to health.

11:9 walks in the day: Jesus can travel safely in Judea so long as his "hour" lies in the future (7:30; 8:20; 10:39).

11:11 fallen asleep: A euphemism for biological death (Mt 27:52; Acts 7:60; 1 Cor 15:6). The disciples take Jesus' words literally, thinking Lazarus has only to be awakened.

11:16 die with him: An obscure statement. It may be that Thomas, like Peter in 13:37, is full of confidence that will prove to be rash when Jesus is later arrested and the disciples scatter for their lives (16:32).

11:17 in the tomb four days: Decisive confirmation of Lazarus' death, since by this time the process of bodily decay was thought to begin in earnest. Martha thus expected the tomb to emit an unpleasant "odor" (11:39). Jews during NT times customarily wrapped the dead with a shroud, tied strips of cloth around their extremities (11:44), and anointed their bodies with fragrant oils and spices (19:39–40). The procedure was not strictly equivalent to embalming, but it helped to delay temporarily the stench of bodily corruption (CCC 627). ● *Allegorically* (*Glossa Ordinaria*), four days in the tomb signifies four stages of spiritual death. Original sin is the first death of the human race; violation of the natural law is the second; violation of the written Law of Moses is the third; and despising the gospel of grace is the fourth. A preview of man's resurrection from this fourfold death is seen as Christ brings Lazarus to life after his four-day entombment.

11:22 even now: Martha's faith fills her with confidence. Although she neither begs nor even asks Jesus to intervene for Lazarus, she knows that God's love is more powerful than death and leaves Jesus to handle the situation as he sees fit.

11:24 the resurrection: A doctrine already current in Judaism (Dan 12:2–3; 2 Mac 7:9). Only the Sadducees denied that our bodies would live again on the last day (Mt 22:23; Acts 23:8). See topical essay: *Who Are the Sadducees?* at Mk 12.

11:25 I am the resurrection: Jesus places all hopes for a future resurrection upon himself. He possesses the absolute sovereignty over life and death that was always believed to be the sole prerogative of Yahweh (1 Sam 2:6; Wis 16:13; CCC 994).

---

x Greek *he.*
y Greek *fifteen stadia.*
z Other ancient authorities omit *and the life.*

Jesus Weeps

28 When she had said this, she went and called her sister Mary, saying quietly, "The Teacher is here and is calling for you." 29And when she heard it, she rose quickly and went to him. 30Now Jesus had not yet come to the village, but was still in the place where Martha had met him. 31When the Jews who were with her in the house, consoling her, saw Mary rise quickly and go out, they followed her, supposing that she was going to the tomb to weep there. 32Then Mary, when she came where Jesus was and saw him, fell at his feet, saying to him, "Lord, if you had been here, my brother would not have died." 33When Jesus saw her weeping, and the Jews who came with her also weeping, he was deeply moved in spirit and troubled; 34and he said, "Where have you laid him?" They said to him, "Lord, come and see." 35Jesus wept. 36So the Jews said, "See how he loved him!" 37But some of them said, "Could not he who opened the eyes of the blind man have kept this man from dying?"

Jesus Raises Lazarus to Life

38 Then Jesus, deeply moved again, came to the tomb; it was a cave, and a stone lay upon it. 39Jesus said, "Take away the stone." Martha, the sister of the dead man, said to him, "Lord, by this time there will be an odor, for he has been dead four days." 40Jesus said to her, "Did I not tell you that if you would believe you would see the glory of God?" 41So they took away the stone. And Jesus lifted up his eyes and said, "Father, I thank you that you have heard me. 42I knew that you always hear me, but I have said this on account of the people standing by, that they may believe that you sent me." 43When he had said this, he cried with a loud voice, "Laz'arus, come out." 44The dead man came out, his hands and feet bound with bandages, and his face wrapped with a cloth. Jesus said to them, "Unbind him, and let him go."

The Plot to Put Jesus to Death

45 Many of the Jews therefore, who had come with Mary and had seen what he did, believed in him; 46but some of them went to the Pharisees and told them what Jesus had done. 47So the chief priests and the Pharisees gathered the council, and said, "What are we to do? For this man performs many signs. 48If we let him go on like this, every one will believe in him, and the Romans will come and destroy both our holy place*a* and our nation." 49But one of them, Cai'aphas, who was high priest that year, said to them, "You know nothing at all; 50you do not understand that it is expedient for you that one man should die for the people, and that the whole nation should not perish." 51He did not say this of his own accord, but being high priest that year he prophesied that Jesus should die for the nation, 52and not for the nation only, but to gather into one the children of God who are scattered abroad. 53So from that day on they took counsel about how to put him to death.

54 Jesus therefore no longer went about openly among the Jews, but went from there to the country near the wilderness, to a town called E'phraim; and there he stayed with the disciples.

55 Now the Passover of the Jews was at hand, and many went up from the country to Jerusalem

---

11:32: Jn 11:22.   **11:35:** Lk 19:41.   **11:37:** Jn 9:7.   **11:38:** Mt 27:60; Mk 15:46; Lk 24:2; Jn 20:1.   **11:41:** Jn 17:1; Mt 11:25.   **11:42:** Jn 12:30.   **11:44:** Jn 19:40; 20:7.   **11:49:** Mt 26:3.   **11:52:** Jn 10:16; 17:21.   **11:55:** Mt 26:1; Mk 14:1; Lk 22:1; Jn 13:1.

11:32 if you had been here: Mary's initial disappointment mirrors that of Martha (11:21).

11:33 troubled: Literally, "angered". Though left unexplained, Jesus is probably angry with the Jews who are now weeping with Mary but who will soon betray him to hostile authorities (11:46). In other words, he foresees that the raising of Lazarus, while strengthening the faith of some, will also occasion the unbelief and treachery of others (11:53; 12:10).

11:35 Jesus wept: Tears, not of despair, but of love and sympathy for Lazarus and his family. This small narrative detail points to an awesome theological mystery: Jesus, who became man in every respect except sin, experienced a full range of human emotions (CCC 478).

11:43 with a loud voice: Dramatizes what will take place at the general resurrection on the last day, when the dead will hear the "voice" of the Son of man and come forth from their tombs to live again (5:25-29; CCC 988-91).

11:47 the council: The Sanhedrin, the supreme court of the Jews. Though many reasons underlie their conspiracy against Jesus (11:53), the raising of Lazarus was particularly insulting to the Sadducees, who did not believe such a thing was possible in the first place (Acts 23:6-8). See notes on 11:24 and Mk 14:55.

11:48 the Romans will come: The statement is brimming with historical irony. The Romans did in fact destroy both Jerusa-

lem and its Temple in A.D. 70, not because the Jewish authorities let Jesus continue his ministry in peace, but precisely because they condemned him to a violent death. In the end, it was not the acceptance of Jesus that threatened the city but the rejection of him that made its demise inevitable (CCC 596-97, 1753). See note on 2:19. **our holy place:** A reference to the Temple or to Jerusalem more generally (Acts 6:13; 21:28).

11:49 Caiaphas: The high priest of Israel from A.D. 18 to 36. As such, he was the recognized head of the Jewish "council" (11:47).

11:51 he prophesied: Caiaphas unwittingly announces that Jesus will die for the salvation of the nation. This is not his own insight, but the grace of prophecy speaking through him in virtue of his priestly office and position as chief teacher of Israel.

11:52 the children of God: Recalls the "other sheep" that Jesus promised to gather into his "one flock" (10:16). It indicates that Christ calls to himself not only Israelites living in the land of Judea, but Israelites and Gentiles who are scattered throughout the Mediterranean world and beyond (Is 43:5-7; 66:18-21; Jer 31:10). The gospel of Christ thus reunifies the human family by gathering believers from every nation into the divine family of God (CCC 706, 2793). See note on 1:12.

11:54 Ephraim: A village of uncertain location, but probably north of Jerusalem in the lower region of Samaria.

11:55 the Passover: The third mention of this feast in John (2:13; 6:4). **to purify themselves:** Jews underwent a process of ritual purification before the Passover, since it was forbidden

---

a Greek *our place.*

before the Passover, to purify themselves. [56]They were looking for Jesus and saying to one another as they stood in the temple, "What do you think? That he will not come to the feast?" [57]Now the chief priests and the Pharisees had given orders that if any one knew where he was, he should let them know, so that they might arrest him.

Mary of Bethany Anoints Jesus

12 Six days before the Passover, Jesus came to Bethany, where Laz´arus was, whom Jesus had raised from the dead. [2]There they made him a supper; Martha served, and Laz´arus was one of those at table with him. [3]Mary took a pound of costly ointment of pure nard and anointed the feet of Jesus and wiped his feet with her hair; and the house was filled with the fragrance of the ointment. [4]But Judas Iscariot, one of his disciples (he who was to betray him), said, [5]"Why was this ointment not sold for three hundred denarii [b] and given to the poor?" [6]This he said, not that he cared for the poor but because he was a thief, and as he had the money box he used to take what was put into it. [7]Jesus said, "Let her alone, let her keep it for the day of my burial. [8]The poor you always have with you, but you do not always have me."

The Plot to Put Lazarus to Death

[9]When the great crowd of the Jews learned that he was there, they came, not only on account of Jesus but also to see Laz´arus, whom he had raised from the dead. [10]So the chief priests planned to put Laz´arus also to death, [11]because on account of him many of the Jews were going away and believing in Jesus.

Jesus' Triumphal Entry into Jerusalem

[12]The next day a great crowd who had come to the feast heard that Jesus was coming to Jerusalem. [13]So they took branches of palm trees and went out to meet him, crying, "Hosanna! Blessed is he who comes in the name of the Lord, even the King of Israel!" [14]And Jesus found a young donkey and sat upon it; as it is written,

[15] "Fear not, daughter of Zion;
   behold, your king is coming,
   sitting on a donkey's colt!"

[16]His disciples did not understand this at first; but when Jesus was glorified, then they remembered that this had been written of him and had been done to him. [17]The crowd that had been with him when he called Laz´arus out of the tomb and raised him from the dead bore witness. [18]The reason why the crowd went to meet him was that they heard he had done this sign. [19]The Pharisees then said to one another, "You see that you can do nothing; look, the world has gone after him."

11:56: Jn 7:11.   **12:1–8:** Mt 26:6–13; Mk 14:3–9; Lk 7:37–38.   **12:4:** Jn 6:71; 13:26.   **12:6:** Lk 8:3.   **12:7:** Jn 19:40.   **12:10:** Mk 14:1.   **12:12–15:** Mt 21:4–9; Mk 11:7–10; Lk 19:35–38.   **12:13:** Ps 118:25; Jn 1:49.   **12:15:** Zech 9:9.   **12:16:** Mk 9:32; Jn 2:22.

---

to celebrate the festival in a state of ceremonial uncleanness (Num 9:9–11; 2 Chron 30:18–21).

12:1–8 The anointing of Jesus at Bethany is also narrated in Mt 26:6–13 and Mk 14:3–9. The episode is similar but distinct from the earlier anointing at the house of Simon the Pharisee in Lk 7:36–50.

12:1 Six days before the Passover: The chronology of the Fourth Gospel places this event on Saturday evening just before Holy Week. The following day is Palm Sunday (12:12).

12:3 pure nard: An imported spice from India. **anointed the feet:** Matthew and Mark have her also anoint the "head" of Jesus (Mt 26:7; Mk 14:3). **the house was filled:** The detail suggests John is testifying to what he himself smelled on the occasion. It may be symbolic of what Jesus says explicitly in the Synoptic tradition: the spread of the fragrance throughout the house anticipates the news of this event spreading throughout the world (Mt 26:13; Mk 14:9).

12:5 three hundred denarii: Nearly an entire year's income for a laborer, since a single denarius was equivalent to a single day's wage (Mt 20:2). It is tragic that Judas complained about Mary's extravagance when he himself betrayed Jesus for much less—a mere "thirty pieces of silver" (Mt 26:15).

12:6 not that he cared: Judas wants to pocket the proceeds of the sale for himself, not to give it away as alms for the needy. **the money box:** Suggests that Judas was the treasurer in charge of the disciples' funds (13:29; Lk 8:3).

12:8 The poor: Jesus is not indifferent toward the poor. Elsewhere he promotes almsgiving in no uncertain terms (Mt 6:2–4; Lk 6:30; 12:33). ● The words of Jesus echo the words of Deut 15:11, which states that the unceasing presence of the poor offers countless opportunities to give generously to less fortunate neighbors. The disciples, too, will have plenty of chances to give alms, but only a brief time remains to be generous toward Jesus while he remains among them (CCC 2449).

12:12 The next day: Palm Sunday. **come to the feast:** Three times a year the nation of Israel traveled to Jerusalem to celebrate the great festivals of Passover, Pentecost, and Tabernacles (Acts 2:5–11). Even Gentiles were known to make the pilgrimage from considerable distances (12:20; Acts 8:27).

12:13 branches of palm: Recalls how the Israelites waved bundles of palm branches for the feast of Tabernacles (Lev 23:40; 2 Mac 10:6–7). **Hosanna!:** A Hebrew acclamation meaning "Save us!" (Ps 118:25). **Blessed . . . name of the Lord:** An excerpt from Ps 118:26, one of the Hallel Psalms (113–118) customarily sung at Israel's great feasts. See note on Mk 11:8–10 and CCC 559.

12:15 Fear not, daughter of Zion: A reference to Zech 9:9. ● Zechariah depicts the royal procession of the Messiah into Jerusalem in a manner that recalls King Solomon's coronation ceremony in 1 Kings 1:38–40. Though a victorious king and leader, he will be mounted on a humble donkey instead of a powerful war horse; indeed, the Messiah will banish the instruments of warfare and proclaim "peace" to Israel and all nations (Zech 9:10). This text provides one of the clearest indications that the Messiah would not be a military general, poised to fight against Israel's political oppressors, but a peaceful king who calls for an end to retaliation and bloodshed.

12:16 they remembered: The Holy Spirit inspired the memory of the apostles not only to recall the prophecies and events of the past, but to understand them in terms of the Father's saving plan (2:22; 14:26).

12:19 the world has gone after him: A sweeping assessment of Jesus' popularity. Since John 7, the evangelist has noted a steady stream of Jews believing in him despite opposition from the Jerusalem authorities (7:31; 8:30; 9:38; 10:42; 11:45).

---

[b] The denarius was a day's wage for a laborer.

Some Greeks Wish to See Jesus

20 Now among those who went up to worship at the feast were some Greeks. ²¹So these came to Philip, who was from Beth-sa´ida in Galilee, and said to him, "Sir, we wish to see Jesus." ²²Philip went and told Andrew; Andrew went with Philip and they told Jesus. ²³And Jesus answered them, "The hour has come for the Son of man to be glorified. ²⁴Truly, truly, I say to you, unless a grain of wheat falls into the earth and dies, it remains alone; but if it dies, it bears much fruit. ²⁵He who loves his life loses it, and he who hates his life in this world will keep it for eternal life. ²⁶If any one serves me, he must follow me; and where I am, there shall my servant be also; if any one serves me, the Father will honor him.

Jesus Speaks about His Death

27 "Now is my soul troubled. And what shall I say? 'Father, save me from this hour'? No, for this purpose I have come to this hour. ²⁸Father, glorify your name." Then a voice came from heaven, "I have glorified it, and I will glorify it again." ²⁹The crowd standing by heard it and said that it had thundered. Others said, "An angel has spoken to him." ³⁰Jesus answered, "This voice has come for your sake, not for mine. ³¹Now is the judgment of this world, now shall the ruler of this world be cast out; ³²and I, when I am lifted up from the earth, will draw all men to myself." ³³He said this to show by what death he was to die. ³⁴The crowd answered

him, "We have heard from the law that the Christ remains for ever. How can you say that the Son of man must be lifted up? Who is this Son of man?" ³⁵Jesus said to them, "The light is with you for a little longer. Walk while you have the light, lest the darkness overtake you; he who walks in the darkness does not know where he goes. ³⁶While you have the light, believe in the light, that you may become sons of light."

The Unbelief of the People

When Jesus had said this, he departed and hid himself from them. ³⁷Though he had done so many signs before them, yet they did not believe in him; ³⁸it was that the word spoken by the prophet Isaiah might be fulfilled:

"Lord, who has believed our report,
and to whom has the arm of the Lord been
     revealed?"

³⁹Therefore they could not believe. For Isaiah again said,

⁴⁰ "He has blinded their eyes and hardened their
     heart,
lest they should see with their eyes and
     perceive with their heart,
and turn for me to heal them."

⁴¹Isaiah said this because he saw his glory and spoke of him. ⁴²Nevertheless many even of the authorities believed in him, but for fear of the Phari-

12:20 some Greeks: Either Gentile converts to Judaism or "God fearers" who were attracted to Judaism but were not circumcised (Acts 13:26; 17:4). Their request for an audience with Jesus anticipates his prophecy that "all men" will be drawn to him (12:32).

12:23 The hour has come: A decisive turning point in the Gospel narrative, when the awaited "hour" of Jesus has finally arrived (2:4; 4:23; 5:25; 7:30; etc.). The inquiry of the Greeks sets this in motion, indicating that the forthcoming suffering of Jesus will secure blessings not only for Israel but for the whole world (1:29; 4:42; 1 Jn 2:2).

12:24 unless a grain of wheat: As a planted seed must decay before it sprouts new life, so Jesus must endure death to bring us eternal life. This principle also holds true for disciples, who must die to themselves to receive the fullness of life from God and be channels of life to others (12:25; 2 Cor 4:11–12).

12:28 a voice: Three times the Father speaks to Jesus from heaven: here, at his Baptism (Mt 3:17), and at his Transfiguration (Mt 17:5). These announcements were made audible for the sake of his followers (12:30).

12:31 ruler of this world: Satan, whose dominion over the world began with Adam's rebellion in the garden (Gen 3:1–19). **cast out:** Christ will *defeat* the devil when he mounts the Cross (Heb 2:14–15) and will *destroy* him when he comes again in glory (Rev 20:10) (CCC 550, 2853).

🛑 **12:32 when I am lifted up:** Refers primarily to the Crucifixion of Christ, as indicated in the next verse, but also hints at his Resurrection and Ascension (CCC 662). See note on 3:14. • The expression recalls the opening line of Isaiah's fourth Servant Song, which runs from Is 52:13 to 53:12. The whole song is a prophetic meditation on the suffering of

the Messiah, who will be exalted and lifted up in the sight of the nations, but only after he is cast down by his own people. Isaiah interprets the humiliation and death of this Servant as a redemptive sacrifice for sin. **draw all men to myself:** Points to the worldwide acceptance of the gospel (Mt 28:18–20; Acts 1:8). • As Isaiah envisioned the Davidic Messiah as an "ensign" posted for the ingathering of the "nations" and the "outcasts of Israel" (Is 11:10–12), so Jesus sees the world gathering around him as he is enthroned on the "sign" of the Cross (CCC 542).

🛑 **12:34 the law:** A reference to the entire OT (10:34; 15:25). • Several passages indicate that the Messiah will reign forever as a priest and king (Ps 110:4; Ezek 37:25; Dan 7:14). **the Son of man:** The royal figure of Dan 7:13. See topical essay: *Jesus, the Son of Man* at Lk 17.

12:36 sons of light: i.e., followers of Jesus, who is the light (1:9; 8:12; 12:46). Paul echoes this teaching in Eph 5:8 and 1 Thess 5:5.

🛑 **12:38 Lord, who has believed:** A quotation from Is 53:1. • Isaiah bemoans the unbelief of Israel, to whom the Messiah comes as a Savior but by whom he is rejected. This is an explicit citation from the same Servant Song to which Jesus made an implicit reference in 12:32.

🛑 **12:40 He has blinded:** A reference to Is 6:10. • Isaiah's mission to Israel in the eighth century B.C. parallels Jesus' mission to Israel in the first century A.D. Both confront a rebellious generation whose unbelief calls down the covenant judgment of Yahweh; and, in both cases, God responds to unbelief by blinding and hardening the rebels, making them unresponsive to the warnings of the Prophets. See note on Mk 4:12.

🛑 **12:41 saw his glory:** Alludes to the context of Is 6:10 cited in the preceding verse. • Isaiah's prophetic mission

sees they did not confess it, lest they should be put out of the synagogue: [43]for they loved the praise of men more than the praise of God.

Summary of Jesus' Teaching

44 And Jesus cried out and said, "He who believes in me, believes not in me but in him who sent me. [45]And he who sees me sees him who sent me. [46]I have come as light into the world, that whoever believes in me may not remain in darkness. [47]If any one hears my sayings and does not keep them, I do not judge him; for I did not come to judge the world but to save the world. [48]He who rejects me and does not receive my sayings has a judge; the word that I have spoken will be his judge on the last day. [49]For I have not spoken on my own authority; the Father who sent me has himself given me commandment what to say and what to speak. [50]And I know that his commandment is eternal life. What I say, therefore, I say as the Father has bidden me."

Jesus Washes the Disciples' Feet

13 Now before the feast of the Passover, when Jesus knew that his hour had come to depart out of this world to the Father, having loved his own who were in the world, he loved them to the end. [2]And during supper, when the devil had already put it into the heart of Judas Iscariot, Simon's son, to betray him, [3]Jesus, knowing that the Father had given all things into his hands, and that he had come from God and was going to God, [4]rose from supper, laid aside his garments, and tied a towel around himself. [5]Then he poured water into a basin, and began to wash the disciples' feet, and to wipe them with the towel that was tied around him. [6]He came to Simon Peter; and Peter said to him, "Lord, do you wash my feet?" [7]Jesus answered him, "What I am doing you do not know now, but afterward you will understand." [8]Peter said to him, "You shall never wash my feet." Jesus answered him, "If I do not wash you, you have no part in me." [9]Simon Peter said to him, "Lord, not my feet only but also my hands and my head!" [10]Jesus said to him, "He who has bathed does not need to wash, except for his feet,[c] but he is clean all over; and you are clean, but not all of you." [11]For he knew who was to betray him; that was why he said, "You are not all clean."

12 When he had washed their feet, and taken his garments, and resumed his place, he said to them, "Do you know what I have done to you? [13]You call me Teacher and Lord; and you are right, for so I am. [14]If I then, your Lord and Teacher, have washed your feet, you also ought to wash one another's feet. [15]For I have given you an example, that you also should do as I have done to you. [16]Truly, truly, I say to you, a servant[d] is not greater than his master; nor is he who is sent greater than he who sent him. [17]If you know these things, blessed are you if you do them. [18]I am not speaking of you all; I know whom I have chosen; it is that the Scripture may be fulfilled, 'He who ate my bread has lifted

---

12:44: Mt 10:40; Jn 5:24.   **12:45:** Jn 14:9.   **12:46:** Jn 1:4; 8:12; 9:5.   **12:47:** Jn 3:17.   **12:48:** Mt 10:14–15.   **13:1:** Jn 11:55; 12:23; 16:28.   **13:2:** Jn 6:71; Mk 14:10.   **13:5:** Lk 7:44; 22:27.   **13:8:** Deut 12:12; Jn 3:5; 9:7.   **13:11:** Jn 13:2.   **13:15:** 1 Pet 2:21.   **13:16:** Mt 10:24; Lk 6:40.   **13:17:** Lk 11:28; Jas 1:25.   **13:18:** Ps 41:9.

---

began with a vision of Yahweh enthroned in glory, "high and lifted up" (Is 6:1). It is possible that John is connecting this with Isaiah's later vision of the messianic Servant, who is likewise "exalted and lifted up" (Is 52:13). The similar wording of these two texts paved the way to a new insight: the *theophany* (vision of Yahweh's glory) of Isaiah 6 is in fact a *Christophany* (vision of the glorified Messiah) (CCC 712–13).

12:44 him who sent me: Because Jesus is the image of the Father (14:9) and speaks the words of the Father (8:28), our response to him is a measure of how we respond to the Father (1 Jn 2:23).

13:1—16:33 Begins the second half of the Gospel, called the "Book of Glory", with four chapters devoted to the final instructions that Jesus gives to the apostles on the night he is betrayed.

13:1 feast of the Passover: The original meaning of this feast, celebrating the passing of the angel of death over the Israelites and their escape from Egypt (Ex 12:13), is being reshaped by the works and words of Christ, who will "pass over" to the Father through the upcoming events of his Passion, Resurrection, and Ascension. This saving work of Jesus will inaugurate a new Exodus, liberating the human family from sin, selfishness, and Satan (1:29; 8:34–36) (CCC 1340). See note on 6:4. **to the end:** i.e., "completely" or "to the fullest extent" (CCC 609).

13:2 during supper: The Synoptic Gospels specify that it was a Passover meal (Mt 26:19; Mk 14:16; Lk 22:15).

13:4 his garments: Symbolic of Christ's human life. John's carefully worded narrative makes this clear: the same Greek

verbs that Jesus uses for laying down his life and taking it up again in 10:17-18 are here employed to describe how Christ "laid aside" his garments (13:4) in service and has "taken" them up again (13:12).

13:5 wash the disciples' feet: A gesture of hospitality normally performed by a household slave, not the presiding host. Jesus thus shows himself a model of humility (1 Tim 5:10) and, at the same time, gives a preview of the heroic service he will render when he accepts the humiliation of the Cross (Mk 10:45; Phil 2:5–8).

13:8 no part in me: Peter cannot be a disciple of Christ on his own terms but must submit himself to the divine plan already determined by the Lord.

13:10 He who has bathed: Seems to imply that the apostles have already been baptized, although this is not explicitly stated in the Gospels. ● Jesus' words hint at the distinction between Baptism, which washes away every stain of sin committed (actual) and contracted (Original), and the Sacrament of Reconciliation, which cleanses us of the accumulated dust of sins committed after our baptismal washing (20:23; 1 Jn 1:9; CCC 1446).

13:15 an example: Jesus says with words what was already expressed in his deeds: we must pattern our lives after Jesus, whose actions show us how to love and honor our heavenly Father (Mt 11:29; CCC 520). Included in this is the willingness to serve others even to the point of death (15:13).

13:16 a servant is not greater: Similar statements occur in Mt 10:24 and Lk 22:27.

13:18 He who ate my bread: A quotation from Ps 41:9. ● The Psalmist laments the treachery of his enemies but even more that of his trusted companion, who ate at his table as

---

[c] Other ancient authorities omit *except for his feet.*
[d] Or *slave.*

When Did Jesus Celebrate the Last Supper?

ONE of the great chronological difficulties in the study of the Gospels is determining the date of the Last Supper. All four Gospels agree that Jesus died on the afternoon of Good Friday a few hours before sundown and the onset of the Jewish Sabbath. What is strange, however, is that the Synoptic Gospels have Jesus celebrating a Passover meal before Good Friday (Mt 26:17-20; Mk 14:12-17; Lk 22:7-16), while John's Gospel tells us that the Passover was not celebrated by the authorities of Jerusalem until the night of Good Friday itself (Jn 18:28; 19:14). What can be made of this apparent discrepancy? How can Jesus have celebrated the Passover *before* his arrest and condemnation (Synoptics) when the Passover did not even begin until several hours *after* his Crucifixion (John)?

Some handle the problem by denying that the Last Supper was truly a Passover meal, even though the Synoptic Gospels assert this. Others insist that Jesus must have chosen to celebrate the feast a day early. Others contend that the Fourth Gospel actually follows the same chronology as the Synoptic Gospels when John's historical notations are read differently. A more promising attempt to unravel this mystery rests upon the diverse makeup of Judaism in the days of Jesus. Although scholars once thought that first-century Judaism was a unified religion followed by all but a few radical sects, it is widely recognized today that the Jews were very much divided. One point of contention between rival communities was the liturgical calendar. The priests and Sadducees who managed the Jerusalem Temple followed a 354-day *lunar* calendar that marked the date of sacred festivals by observing the cycles of the moon. When the Dead Sea Scrolls were unearthed in the middle of the 20th century, the world was astonished to discover that the Essene Jews of Qumran, in direct opposition to the Temple system, followed a 364-day *solar* calendar instead. This meant that while Passover fell on a different day of the week each year according to the lunar calendar of the Temple, the Essene solar calendar was arranged so that feast days always fell on the same day of the week year after year. For them, Passover was always celebrated on a Tuesday night (the Jews considered this the first part of Wednesday). Could Jesus have followed the Essene calendar instead of the Temple calendar when he celebrated the Passover with his disciples? Is there any evidence that the Last Supper took place on Tuesday night of Holy Week instead of Thursday night? Several scholars have answered "yes" to both of these questions, and their findings are worth our consideration.

1. ARCHAEOLOGY

Recent excavations suggest that a community of Essene Jews lived just inside the walls of Jerusalem during the first century A.D. This Essene settlement was located on the southwestern hill of the city (modern Mt. Zion). Interestingly, this is the same quarter of the city where Christian tradition locates the site of the upper room (cenacle). Perhaps Jesus, aware that his death would prevent him from celebrating the Passover according to the Temple calendar, decided to celebrate the feast earlier in the week when it was observed by the Essene community. The traditional location of the upper room within the Essene quarter of Jerusalem makes this a distinct possibility.

2. CHRONOLOGY

The hypothesis that Jesus celebrated the Last Supper on Tuesday evening has the added benefit of solving another chronological difficulty. The Synoptic Gospels say that Christ was anointed at Bethany "two days" before the Passover (Mk 14:1), whereas the Fourth Gospel says the event took place "six days" before the Passover (Jn 12:1). This discrepancy disappears if the Synoptics are referring to the Tuesday evening Essene Passover and John is referring to the Friday evening Temple Passover. Moreover, the hypothesis that Jesus celebrated the feast on Tuesday night rather than Thursday night would allow more adequate time for the extensive legal proceedings with Annas (Jn 18:13, 19-23), Caiaphas (Jn 18:24), the Sanhedrin (Lk 22:66-71), Herod (Lk 23:6-11), and Pilate (Jn 18:28-40) that took place between his arrest and condemnation.

3. TRADITION

Another consideration comes from the ancient Church. A Syriac document from the second or third century states explicitly that Jesus celebrated the Last Supper on Tuesday night (*Didascalia Apostolorum* 5, 12-18). A similar tradition preserved by the third-century bishop Victorinus of Pettau (*De Fabrica Mundi* 3), as well as the fourth-century bishop Saint Epiphanius (*Panarion* 51, 26), states that Jesus was taken into custody on Tuesday night (i.e., early Wednesday). The *Didascalia* and Victorinus explain this as the reason why Wednesdays and Fridays were days of fasting and penance in the early Church, for these two days marked the beginning and end of Christ's historical Passion (*Didache* 8, 1). It is possible (but not certain) that the commemoration of Holy Thursday so familiar today originated as an interpretive tradition deduced from a reading of the Synoptic Gospels. The Synoptics do indeed give the "impression" that Jesus celebrated the Passover on the eve of Good Friday, yet the evangelists do not state this explicitly. The commemoration of Holy Tuesday, on the other hand, may represent a historical tradition in the strict sense, since it is difficult to imagine how such a strange understanding of Jesus' final days could have circulated and survived for so long unless it had some claim to historical authenticity.

In the end, it must be admitted that all of this amounts to a working hypothesis, which, like every hypothesis, is subject to revision or even rejection when the evidence requires it. Further information may indeed come to light to disprove this tentative proposal and substantiate the tradition of Holy Thursday instead. For the present time, however, the cumulative force of these archaeological, chronological, and traditional findings do more to ease the chronological tension between the Synoptic Gospels and the Fourth Gospel than alternative proposals. At the very least, they cause us to recognize that Passover was celebrated at two different times (Tuesday and Friday night) and at two different locations (the Essene quarter and the rest of Jerusalem) in the year that Jesus died. Putting the Last Supper on Tuesday night is consistent with this situation and may prove to be the best solution that biblical and historical scholarship presently has to offer on this question. «

his heel against me.' ¹⁹I tell you this now, before it takes place, that when it does take place you may believe that I am he. ²⁰Truly, truly, I say to you, he who receives any one whom I send receives me; and he who receives me receives him who sent me."

Jesus Foretells His Betrayal

21 When Jesus had thus spoken, he was troubled in spirit, and testified, "Truly, truly, I say to you, one of you will betray me." ²²The disciples looked at one another, uncertain of whom he spoke. ²³One of his disciples, whom Jesus loved, was lying close to the breast of Jesus; ²⁴so Simon Peter beckoned to him and said, "Tell us who it is of whom he speaks." ²⁵So lying thus, close to the breast of Jesus, he said to him, "Lord, who is it?" ²⁶Jesus answered, "It is he to whom I shall give this morsel when I have dipped it." So when he had dipped the morsel, he gave it to Judas, the son of Simon Iscariot. ²⁷Then after the morsel, Satan entered into him. Jesus said to him, "What you are going to do, do quickly." ²⁸Now no one at the table knew why he said this to him. ²⁹Some thought that, because Judas had the money box, Jesus was telling him, "Buy what we need for the feast"; or, that he should give something to the poor. ³⁰So, after receiving the morsel, he immediately went out; and it was night.

The New Commandment

31 When he had gone out, Jesus said, "Now is the Son of man glorified, and in him God is glorified; ³²if God is glorified in him, God will also glorify him in himself, and glorify him at once. ³³Little children, yet a little while I am with you. You will seek me; and as I said to the Jews so now I say to you, 'Where I am going you cannot come.' ³⁴A new commandment I give to you, that you love one another; even as I have loved you, that you also love one another. ³⁵By this all men will know that you are my disciples, if you have love for one another."

Jesus Foretells Peter's Denial

36 Simon Peter said to him, "Lord, where are you going?" Jesus answered, "Where I am going you cannot follow me now; but you shall follow afterward." ³⁷Peter said to him, "Lord, why can I not follow you now? I will lay down my life for you." ³⁸Jesus answered, "Will you lay down your life for me? Truly, truly, I say to you, the cock will not crow, till you have denied me three times.

Jesus the Way, the Truth, and the Life

14 "Let not your hearts be troubled; believe*ᵉ* in God, believe also in me. ²In my Father's house are many rooms; if it were not so, would I have told you that I go to prepare a place for you? ³And when I go and prepare a place for you, I will come again and will take you to myself, that where I am you may be also. ⁴And you know the way where I am going."*ᶠ* ⁵Thomas said to him, "Lord, we do not know where you are going; how can we know the way?" ⁶Jesus said to him, "I am the way, and the truth, and the life; no one comes to the Father, but by me. ⁷If you had known me, you would have known my Father also; henceforth you know him and have seen him."

8 Philip said to him, "Lord, show us the Father, and we shall be satisfied." ⁹Jesus said to him, "Have I been with you so long, and yet you do not know

---

13:19: Jn 14:29; 8:28.   **13:20:** Mt 10:40; Lk 10:16.   **13:21-26:** Mt 26:21-25; Mk 14:18-21; Lk 22:21-23.   **13:23:** Jn 19:26; 20:2; 21:7, 20.   **13:26:** Jn 6:71.   **13:29:** Jn 12:6.   **13:30:** Lk 22:53.   **13:31-32:** Jn 17:1.   **13:33:** 1 Jn 2:1; Jn 7:33.   **13:34:** Jn 15:12, 17; 1 Jn 3:23; 2 Jn 5; Lev 19:18; 1 Thess 4:9; 1 Pet 1:22; Heb 13:1; Eph 5:2; 1 Jn 4:10.   **13:36:** Jn 21:18; 2 Pet 1:14.   **13:37-38:** Mt 26:33-35; Mk 14:29-31; Lk 22:33-34.   **14:2:** Jn 13:33.   **14:5:** Jn 11:16.   **14:6:** Jn 10:9; 1:4, 14.

---

a friend only to betray him as a foe. As the psalm progresses, however, the turmoil of the Psalmist gives way to the confidence that Yahweh will vindicate him in due time (Ps 41:11-12).

13:19 believe that I am: The foreknowledge of Jesus is further evidence that he is God from true God, the true "I AM". See note on 6:20.

13:22 uncertain of whom: Judas successfully camouflages his malice from the other disciples.

13:23 whom Jesus loved: i.e., the Apostle John. See introduction: *Author.* **lying close:** Festal meals were eaten, not in a sitting position, but in a reclining position on cushions spread around a short table. See note on Lk 7:36.

13:27 after the morsel, Satan: Although Judas is sharing a meal with Jesus, he is feeding on the lies of the devil (8:44). The darkness that fills him draws him out into the "night" (13:30).

13:31 God is glorified: It is precisely when Christ accepts his suffering at the hands of evil men that he shows us the dimensions of God's love for the world (Rom 5:8; Jn 3:16).

13:34 new commandment: The Torah commanded *human* love for ourselves and our neighbor (Lev 19:18). Jesus commands *divine* love for one another that is modeled on his own acts of charity and generosity (15:13; 1 Jn 3:16-18). This super-

natural love comes not from us but from the Spirit (Rom 5:5; CCC 1822-29). See note on 1 Cor 13:4-7.

13:37 lay down my life: Peter is probably sincere but certainly overconfident. Soon his bravery will be crushed under the weight of human fear (18:25-27).

14:1 Let not your hearts: Jesus wants to protect his disciples from despair at his death and from discouragement when persecution comes their way (14:27; 16:33). Only the peace of God that surpasses understanding can calm their anxieties (Phil 4:6-7).

14:2 my Father's house: A similar expression is used in 2:16 for the Jerusalem Temple, hinting that the Father's house is a heavenly sanctuary (Rev 21:22) perched high above in the heavenly Jerusalem (Gal 4:26; Rev 21:1). This is the eternal dwelling where the glorified angels and saints worship the Lord in the eternal liturgy (Heb 12:22-24; Rev 4-5) (CCC 2795). **many rooms:** Similar to the Herodian Temple in Jerusalem, which had several courts for worship, chambers for storage, and living quarters for priests.

14:6 I am the way: A claim to be the sole Savior of the world (Acts 4:12). He is the one mediator chosen by the Father to bring the human family to glory. Earlier Jesus made this claim when he compared himself to Jacob's ladder (1:51) (CCC 661, 2466).

14:9 has seen the Father: Jesus is the visible image of the invisible God (Col 1:15), his human flesh (1:14) being an icon

---

ᵉ Or *you believe.*
ᶠ Other ancient authorities read *where I am going you know, and the way you know.*

me, Philip? He who has seen me has seen the Father; how can you say, 'Show us the Father'? ¹⁰Do you not believe that I am in the Father and the Father in me? The words that I say to you I do not speak on my own authority; but the Father who dwells in me does his works. ¹¹Believe me that I am in the Father and the Father in me; or else believe me for the sake of the works themselves.

12 "Truly, truly, I say to you, he who believes in me will also do the works that I do; and greater works than these will he do, because I go to the Father. ¹³Whatever you ask in my name, I will do it, that the Father may be glorified in the Son; ¹⁴if you ask*ᵍ* anything in my name, I will do it.

The Promise of the Holy Spirit

15 "If you love me, you will keep my commandments. ¹⁶And I will ask the Father, and he will give you another Counselor, to be with you for ever, ¹⁷even the Spirit of truth, whom the world cannot receive, because it neither sees him nor knows him; you know him, for he dwells with you, and will be in you.

18 "I will not leave you desolate; I will come to you. ¹⁹Yet a little while, and the world will see me no more, but you will see me; because I live, you will live also. ²⁰In that day you will know that I am in my Father, and you in me, and I in you. ²¹He who has my commandments and keeps them, he it is who loves me; and he who loves me will be loved by my Father, and I will love him and manifest myself to him." ²²Judas (not Iscariot) said to him, "Lord, how is it that you will manifest yourself to us, and not to the world?" ²³Jesus answered him, "If a man loves me, he will keep my word, and my Father will love him, and we will come to him and make our home with him. ²⁴He who does not love me does not keep my words; and the word which you hear is not mine but the Father's who sent me.

25 "These things I have spoken to you, while I am still with you. ²⁶But the Counselor, the Holy Spirit, whom the Father will send in my name, he will teach you all things, and bring to your remembrance all that I have said to you. ²⁷Peace I leave with you; my peace I give to you; not as the world gives do I give to you. Let not your hearts be troubled, neither let them be afraid. ²⁸You heard me

---

14:9: Jn 12:45. **14:11:** Jn 10:38. **14:13:** Mt 7:7; Jn 15:7, 16; 16:23; Jas 1:5. **14:15:** Jn 15:10; 1 Jn 5:3; 2 Jn 6.
14:16: Jn 14:26; 15:26; 16:7; 1 Jn 2:1. **14:19:** Jn 7:33. **14:22:** Acts 1:13; 10:40–41. **14:23:** 1 Jn 2:24; Rev 21:3.
14:27: Jn 16:33; Phil 4:7; Col 3:15; Jn 20:19.

---

of divine spirit (4:24). Through faith we see how Christ's entire life shows us the heart of the Father and his love for the world (3:16; 5:19–23; CCC 516).

14:13 Whatever you ask: The Ascension of Jesus will not be his retirement, since even now he lives to make priestly intercession for the Church on earth (Heb 7:25; 9:24). **I will do it:** A promise to grant whatever is needed to facilitate our salvation (Mt 7:7-11). To pray in the name of Jesus is to pray that the Father will bless us through him (16:23–24; CCC 2614, 2615).

14:15 If you love me: Our commitment to Christ is proved by works and not merely by words (14:23–24; 1 Jn 3:18).

14:17 with you . . . in you: The first expression refers to the Spirit's *ecclesial* presence within the Church as a whole, and the second to his *personal* presence dwelling within each of God's children individually. For this reason both the universal Church (Eph 2:19–22) and individual Christians (1 Cor 6:19) can be called "temples" of the Spirit (CCC 797).

14:18 desolate: Literally, "orphans". **I will come to you:** i.e., with the Father and the Spirit (14:23). ● When Jesus withdraws his visible presence from the world, he does not withdraw his spiritual presence. Christ is always present in his Church, especially in the liturgy, where he ministers through his priests, speaks through the Scriptures, and sanctifies us through the sacraments (CCC 788, 1380).

14:22 Judas (not Iscariot): Presumably "Judas the son of James" (Lk 6:16), also called "Thaddaeus" (Mt 10:3). See chart: *The Twelve Apostles* at Mk 3.

14:23 our home with him: Through grace the living presence of the Trinity inhabits the hearts of the faithful (14:17; Gal 2:20). From John's perspective, God dwells in the saints on earth before the saints dwell with God in heaven (14:2-3; Rev 21:22; CCC 260).

14:26 the Holy Spirit: Sent from heaven to complete the teaching ministry of Jesus and give the apostles an accurate understanding of the gospel (16:12-13). The Spirit also works through the sacraments to renew the world with the graces and

blessings that Christ died to give us (3:5; 6:63; 20:22–23) (CCC 243, 729). See note on 16:13. **teach you . . . bring to your remembrance:** The terms "you" and "your" in this verse are plural. It is thus a promise to guide and instruct the ordained leaders of the Church, here represented by the eleven apostles. It is not a promise that the Spirit will grant every individual Christian supernatural insight into the full meaning of the gospel or the Scriptures (2 Pet 1:20–21).

14:27 my peace: Not worldly peace, which is often procured by violence and is always unstable, but a spiritual serenity that comforts us regardless of our outward circumstances. See word study: *Peace* at Col 3.

14:28 the Father is greater: The Son is equal to the Father in his divinity but less than the Father in his humanity. ● Although no one of the Divine Persons exceeds the oth-

---

WORD STUDY

Counselor (14:16)

Paraklētos (Gk.): an "advocate" or "helper". The word is used five times in John's writings, always with reference to Jesus or the Holy Spirit. It is a legal term for an attorney or spokesman who defends the cause of the accused in a courtroom. Jesus uses it for a heavenly intercessor who is called to the side of God's children to offer strength and support. Jesus is a "Paraclete" because in heaven he pleads to the Father for believers still struggling on earth (1 Jn 2:1). The Spirit, too, is a "Paraclete" because he is sent to strengthen the disciples in Jesus' absence (Jn 14:16), instruct them in the truth (Jn 14:26; 15:26), and defend them against the prosecutions of the devil (16:7–11), who is the "accuser" of the family of God (Rev 12:10).

ᵍ Other ancient authorities add me.

say to you, 'I go away, and I will come to you.' If you loved me, you would have rejoiced, because I go to the Father; for the Father is greater than I. [29]And now I have told you before it takes place, so that when it does take place, you may believe. [30]I will no longer talk much with you, for the ruler of this world is coming. He has no power over me; [31]but I do as the Father has commanded me, so that the world may know that I love the Father. Rise, let us go from here.

Jesus the True Vine

15 "I am the true vine, and my Father is the vinedresser. [2]Every branch of mine that bears no fruit, he takes away, and every branch that does bear fruit he prunes, that it may bear more fruit. [3]You are already made clean by the word which I have spoken to you. [4]Abide in me, and I in you. As the branch cannot bear fruit by itself, unless it abides in the vine, neither can you, unless you abide in me. [5]I am the vine, you are the branches. He who abides in me, and I in him, he it is that bears much fruit, for apart from me you can do nothing. [6]If a man does not abide in me, he is cast forth as a branch and withers; and the branches are gathered, thrown into the fire and burned. [7]If you abide in me, and my words abide in you, ask whatever you will, and it shall be done for you. [8]By this

my Father is glorified, that you bear much fruit, and so prove to be my disciples. [9]As the Father has loved me, so have I loved you; abide in my love. [10]If you keep my commandments, you will abide in my love, just as I have kept my Father's commandments and abide in his love. [11]These things I have spoken to you, that my joy may be in you, and that your joy may be full.

12 "This is my commandment, that you love one another as I have loved you. [13]Greater love has no man than this, that a man lay down his life for his friends. [14]You are my friends if you do what I command you. [15]No longer do I call you servants,[h] for the servant[i] does not know what his master is doing; but I have called you friends, for all that I have heard from my Father I have made known to you. [16]You did not choose me, but I chose you and appointed you that you should go and bear fruit and that your fruit should abide; so that whatever you ask the Father in my name, he may give it to you. [17]This I command you, to love one another.

The World's Hatred

18 "If the world hates you, know that it has hated me before it hated you. [19]If you were of the world, the world would love its own; but because you are not of the world, but I chose you out of the world, therefore the world hates you. [20]Remember

---

14:29: Jn 13:19.   **14:30:** Jn 12:31.   **14:31:** Mk 14:42; Jn 18:1.   **15:1:** Is 5:1–7; Ezek 19:10; Mk 12:1–9; Mt 15:13; Rom 11:17.   **15:3:** Jn 13:10.   **15:4:** Jn 6:56; 1 Jn 2:6.   **15:7:** Jn 14:13; 16:23; Mt 7:7; Jas 1:5.   **15:8:** Mt 5:16.   **15:10:** Jn 14:15; 1 Jn 5:3.   **15:12:** Jn 13:34.   **15:13:** Rom 5:7; Jn 10:11.   **15:14:** Lk 12:4.   **15:16:** Jn 6:70; 13:18; 14:13; 16:23.   **15:18:** Jn 7:7; 1 Jn 3:13; Mt 10:22; 24:9.   **15:20:** Jn 13:16; Mt 10:24; 1 Cor 4:12; Acts 4:17; 1 Pet 4:14; Rev 2:3.

---

ers in greatness or glory in the eternal Trinity, there is a relational hierarchy among them, where, unlike the Son and the Spirit, the Father alone possesses divine Paternity and has the distinction of being entirely without origin.

14:30 ruler of this world: Satan. See note on 12:31.

14:31 I love the Father: This is the only place in the Gospels where Jesus verbalizes his love for the Father. The fact is never in doubt, however, since his every deed is done to honor the Father (8:29; 15:10), and he will soon make a loving gift of himself to the Father on the Cross (15:13) (CCC 606). ● Christ reveals through his humanity the mystery of his divinity. The life and death of Jesus are thus a visible expression of the invisible life of the Trinity, where the Son eternally pours himself out in love to the Father.

15:1–11 The metaphor of the vine underscores Jesus' union with the disciples and their absolute dependency on him for life and growth. It assumes that because the vinedresser (the Father) seeks an abundant harvest, he trims back the vine stock (Jesus) to rid it of fruitless branches (apostates) and to invigorate the other branches (disciples) to become even more fruitful. ● Several times the OT depicts Israel as a vineyard planted and tended by the Lord (Ps 80:8–16; Is 5:1–7; 27:2–6; Jer 2:21). When Jesus clothes himself with this same imagery, he is stressing that Israel finds its life and vigor no longer in the Old Covenant but in the New Covenant ratified by its Messiah. ● The delivery of this sermon during the Last Supper gives it a sacramental coloring. Note how the invitation to "abide" in Christ (15:4–5) recalls the same notion in the Bread of Life discourse (6:56) and how the Synoptic Gospels make an explicit link between the "fruit of the vine" and the eucharistic meal (Mt 26:29; Mk 14:25; Lk 22:18) (CCC 787).

15:2 he prunes: The Father must trim away our selfishness to increase our growth in love. Pruning probably refers to the trials and fatherly discipline we experience in this life (Heb 12:5–11; Jas 1:2–4; 1 Pet 1:6–7).

15:5 bears much fruit: The fruits of righteousness are borne in us by the Spirit (Gal 5:22–23; CCC 737). Without this life-giving sap, which flows into the branches through the vine, we can do absolutely nothing to please the Father or move closer to salvation (CCC 308, 2074).

15:6 thrown into the fire: Damnation awaits every branch that withers away from Christ and becomes worthless (Mt 3:10; Heb 6:4–8). ● Ezekiel similarly described the residents of Jerusalem as vine branches that failed to yield *fruit* and so became *fuel* for the fires of divine judgment (Ezek 15:1–8). Vines, the prophet reasoned, are useless to the craftsman as wood and thus have no value apart from the grapes they bear.

15:10 my Father's commandments: Love for the Father expresses itself through obeying his commandments as Jesus did (1 Jn 3:23–24). It was common in ancient society for younger siblings to look up to the eldest brother for guidance on how to honor and obey one's parents.

15:13 Greater love: The fullest expression of love consists in pouring out our lives to God as Jesus Christ did on the Cross (1 Jn 3:16). See notes on 13:34 and 14:31.

15:14 my friends: The promise of intimacy with Jesus is conditional because it can be fulfilled only if we commit ourselves to his teaching. ● Abraham, the man of faith, was the first to be called a "friend" of God in the Bible (2 Chron 20:7; Is 41:8).

15:18–27 Jesus cautions the disciples against the hostility and persecution of the world. The hatred it has for Jesus will likewise fall on them for preaching his gospel and living as he lived. The wording of 15:24–25 and 16:2 suggests that by "world" Jesus is referring to unbelieving Israel. See note on 1:10.

---

[h] Or *slaves*.   [i] Or *slave*.

the word that I said to you, 'A servant[i] is not greater than his master.' If they persecuted me, they will persecute you; if they kept my word, they will keep yours also. [21]But all this they will do to you on my account, because they do not know him who sent me. [22]If I had not come and spoken to them, they would not have sin; but now they have no excuse for their sin. [23]He who hates me hates my Father also. [24]If I had not done among them the works which no one else did, they would not have sin; but now they have seen and hated both me and my Father. [25]It is to fulfil the word that is written in their law, 'They hated me without a cause.' [26]But when the Counselor comes, whom I shall send to you from the Father, even the Spirit of truth, who proceeds from the Father, he will bear witness to me; [27]and you also are witnesses, because you have been with me from the beginning.

16 [1]"I have said all this to you to keep you from falling away. [2]They will put you out of the synagogues; indeed, the hour is coming when whoever kills you will think he is offering service to God. [3]And they will do this because they have not known the Father, nor me. [4]But I have said these things to you, that when their hour comes you may remember that I told you of them.

The Work of the Spirit

"I did not say these things to you from the beginning, because I was with you. [5]But now I am going to him who sent me; yet none of you asks me, 'Where are you going?' [6]But because I have said these things to you, sorrow has filled your hearts. [7]Nevertheless I tell you the truth: it is to your advantage that I go away, for if I do not go away, the Counselor will not come to you; but if I go, I will send him to you. [8]And when he comes, he will convince the world of sin and of righteousness and of judgment: [9]of sin, because they do not believe in me; [10]of righteousness, because I go to the Father, and you will see me no more; [11]of judgment, because the ruler of this world is judged.

12 "I have yet many things to say to you, but you cannot bear them now. [13]When the Spirit of truth comes, he will guide you into all the truth; for he will not speak on his own authority, but whatever he hears he will speak, and he will declare to you the things that are to come. [14]He will glorify me, for he will take what is mine and declare it to you. [15]All that the Father has is mine; therefore I said that he will take what is mine and declare it to you.

Sorrow Will Turn into Joy

16 "A little while, and you will see me no more; again a little while, and you will see me." [17]Some of his disciples said to one another, "What is this that he says to us, 'A little while, and you will not see me, and again a little while, and you will see me'; and, 'because I go to the Father'?" [18]They said, "What does he mean by 'a little while'? We do not

---

15:22: Jn 9:41.   **15:25:** Ps 35:19; 69:4.   **15:26:** Jn 14:16, 26; 16:7; 1 Jn 2:1; 5:7.   **15:27:** Jn 19:35; 21:24; 1 Jn 4:14.
16:2: Jn 9:22; Acts 26:9–11; Is 66:5.   **16:5:** Jn 7:33; 14:5.   **16:7:** Jn 14:16, 26; 15:26.   **16:9:** Jn 15:22.
16:10: Acts 3:14; 7:52; 1 Pet 3:18.   **16:11:** Jn 12:31.   **16:14:** Jn 7:39.   **16:16–24:** Jn 14:18–24.

15:22 no excuse: Revelation entails the responsibility of embracing it. Had Jesus not spoken the truth to the world, its culpability would be lessened; since he did, however, scoffers and unbelievers face the dreadful consequences of rejecting the voice of the living God (12:47–50).

15:25 their law: Refers to the entire OT, not only to the Pentateuch (10:34; 12:34). **They hated me:** Echoes Ps 35:19 and 69:4. ● In both verses the Psalmist pleads for Yahweh's vindication because wicked men harass him for no justifiable reason. The disciples must learn from this word of caution from Jesus that the world's hatred will not go unnoticed by the Father, but he will one day deliver them from the malice of their oppressors.

15:26 whom I shall send: The Spirit comes forth from the Father (14:16, 26) and the Son (16:7). ● The mission of the Spirit in history is a reflection of the procession of the Spirit in eternity. This is expressed in the Nicene Creed, which says that the Holy Spirit "proceeds from the Father and the Son" (CCC 244–48).

16:2 out of the synagogues: i.e., excommunicated from the fellowship of Israel. **service to God:** Or "worship to God". According to rabbinic meditations on the Phinehas episode of Num 25:1–13, to slay apostates from Judaism is to sacrifice unto the Lord.

16:5 Where are you going?: Although both Peter (13:36) and Thomas (14:5) asked this question earlier, they were too troubled by the prospect of Jesus' departure to press for information about his destination.

16:7 to your advantage: Greater blessings will come when the Spirit dwells *within* them at Pentecost (14:17; Acts 2:1–4). Chief among these benefits will be the power (1) to proclaim

the gospel with boldness (Acts 1:8; 4:31), (2) to preserve and understand the truth in its fullness (16:13), (3) to give witness to Jesus in times of persecution (Lk 12:11–12), and (4) to fulfil the just requirements of God's Law (Rom 8:4).

16:8 he will convince: The Spirit exposes the sin of unbelief for what it is (3:20), convinces the world that Christ, though condemned as a criminal, was truly righteous (8:46), and makes it known that Satan and every enemy of Christ will face judgment for rejecting him (5:26–29; 12:31; CCC 388, 1433). The mission of the Spirit, here described in juridical language, shows that while he acts as an advocate or defense lawyer for the disciples, he is also a prosecutor who indicts the unbelieving world. See word study: *Counselor* at Jn 14.

16:13 he will guide you: The work of the Spirit counteracts the work of Satan. The former discloses the full meaning of the gospel (14:26); the latter spreads deception and falsehood throughout the world (8:44). The point here is that the Spirit continues the teaching mission of Jesus to bear witness to the truth (8:31–32; 18:37; CCC 687). ● Vatican II outlined the doctrine of magisterial infallibility, meaning that the pope alone or the pope and the bishops united with him are divinely protected from teaching error when they define matters pertaining to faith and morals (*Lumen Gentium*, 25). The guidance of the Spirit is Christ's guarantee that the gospel will not be corrupted, distorted, or misunderstood by the ordained shepherds of the Church during her earthly pilgrimage (CCC 768, 889–92). See note on 14:26.

16:15 declare it to you: The Spirit gives us a share in the divine life and authority of Jesus (6:63; Rom 8:14–16; CCC 690).

16:18 A little while: The disciples will again see Jesus at his Resurrection (20:19–30), and after his Ascension they will await his visible return in glory (Acts 1:9–11).

---

[i] Or *slave*.

know what he means." ¹⁹Jesus knew that they wanted to ask him; so he said to them, "Is this what you are asking yourselves, what I meant by saying, 'A little while, and you will not see me, and again a little while, and you will see me'? ²⁰Truly, truly, I say to you, you will weep and lament, but the world will rejoice; you will be sorrowful, but your sorrow will turn into joy. ²¹When a woman is in labor, she has pain, because her hour has come; but when she is delivered of the child, she no longer remembers the anguish, for joy that a child *ʲ* is born into the world. ²²So you have sorrow now, but I will see you again and your hearts will rejoice, and no one will take your joy from you. ²³In that day you will ask nothing of me. Truly, truly, I say to you, if you ask anything of the Father, he will give it to you in my name. ²⁴Until now you have asked nothing in my name; ask, and you will receive, that your joy may be full.

Peace for the Disciples

25 "I have said this to you in figures; the hour is coming when I shall no longer speak to you in figures but tell you plainly of the Father. ²⁶In that day you will ask in my name; and I do not say to you that I shall ask the Father for you; ²⁷for the Father himself loves you, because you have loved me and have believed that I came from the Father.

²⁸I came from the Father and have come into the world; again, I am leaving the world and going to the Father."

29 His disciples said, "Ah, now you are speaking plainly, not in any figure! ³⁰Now we know that you know all things, and need none to question you; by this we believe that you came from God." ³¹Jesus answered them, "Do you now believe? ³²The hour is coming, indeed it has come, when you will be scattered, every man to his home, and will leave me alone; yet I am not alone, for the Father is with me. ³³I have said this to you, that in me you may have peace. In the world you have tribulation; but be of good cheer, I have overcome the world."

Jesus Prays for the Church

17 When Jesus had spoken these words, he lifted up his eyes to heaven and said, "Father, the hour has come; glorify your Son that the Son may glorify you, ²since you have given him power over all flesh, to give eternal life to all whom you have given him. ³And this is eternal life, that they know you the only true God, and Jesus Christ whom you have sent. ⁴I glorified you on earth, having accomplished the work which you gave me to do; ⁵and now, Father, glorify me in your own presence with the glory which I had with you before the world was made.

16:20: Jn 20:20. **16:21:** Is 13:8; Hos 13:13; Mic 4:9; 1 Thess 5:3. **16:24:** Jn 14:14; 15 11. **16:25:** Jn 10:6; Mt 13:34. **16:32:** Jn 4:23; Lk 14:27; Zech 13:7. **16:33:** Jn 14:27; 15:18; Rom 8:37; 2 Cor 2:14; Rev 3:21. **17:1:** Jn 11:41; 13:31. **17:5:** Jn 1:1; 8:58; Phil 2:6.

16:21 her hour has come: The hour of Christ's Passion is compared to the pangs of childbirth. The disciples, like a woman in labor, will experience extreme distress that soon gives way to joy when Christ is reborn to a new life on Easter morning. • The Prophets similarly compare times of divine testing and judgment to the onset of labor pain (Is 13:6–8; 26:17; Mic 4:10).

16:23 ask nothing . . . ask anything: Two different Greek verbs are translated "ask" in this verse: the first means "to question", and the second "to request". So the disciples must not interrogate Jesus when they see him risen, but they may petition the Father for their needs (CCC 2614).

16:25 in figures: Refers back to the metaphor of the true vine (15:1–6) and probably to numerous parables in the Synoptic Gospels that tell us about the Father (Mt 21:33–41; 22:1–14; Lk 13:6–9).

16:30 you know all things: Amounts to a confession of faith in the divinity of Jesus, since only God is omniscient (21:17; Ps 139:1–6).

16:32 you will be scattered: Jesus foretells his abandonment with the help of Zech 13:7 in the Synoptic Gospels (Mt 26:31; Mk 14:27). His words come to fulfillment with his arrest in Gethsemane (Mk 14:50).

17:1–26 The high priestly prayer of Jesus, who turns attention from his disciples (chaps. 13–16) to his heavenly Father (chap. 17). The prayer has three parts: Jesus offers up his approaching sacrifice to the Father (17:1–5), pleads for the preservation of his disciples (17:6–19), and prays for the unity of the universal Church (17:20–26). This is the longest extended prayer recorded in the Gospels (CCC 2746–51).

17:1 lifted up his eyes: A traditional prayer gesture (Ps 123:1; Mk 6:41). **the hour:** The time of Christ's Passion begins in earnest. Because it involves his rejection and the aggressive

assault of the devil, it is also called the hour of "darkness" (Lk 22:53). See topical essay: *The "Hour" of Jesus* at Jn 4.

17:3 eternal life: To possess life is to "know" the living God in his triune glory. Although this knowledge has a cognitive and intellectual dimension, it also includes a relational bond of love, friendship, and communion with God that grows steadily until our union with him is complete in heaven (Eph 1:17; 1 Jn 4:7). • Personal knowledge of God is a sign of the New Covenant, according to Jer 31:33–34. **the only true God:** The NT doctrine that God is a Trinity is built on the OT doctrine that Yahweh alone is God (Deut 6:4; 32:39). This

WORD STUDY

Glorify (17:1)

Doxazō (Gk.): to "praise", "honor", or "give glory". The verb is used 23 times in John and 38 times in the rest of the NT. From a biblical perspective, the glory of God is the weight and magnificence of his Being (2 Cor 4:17). John shows that Jesus, the eternal Son, possesses the divine glory of his Father (1:14). This glory shines through his miracles (2:11) and especially through his loving acceptance of the Cross (12:23–24). The Son's obedience to his mission glorifies the Father (13:31; 14:13), and in return, the Father glorifies the Son (8:54; 11:4). Before his death, Jesus petitions the Father to glorify his humanity that it may rise again to participate in the eternal glory that he already possesses in his divinity (17:5, 24).

---

*ʲ Greek *a human being*.

6 "I have manifested your name to the men whom you gave me out of the world; they were yours, and you gave them to me, and they have kept your word. [7]Now they know that everything that you have given me is from you; [8]for I have given them the words which you gave me, and they have received them and know in truth that I came from you; and they have believed that you sent me. [9]I am praying for them; I am not praying for the world but for those whom you have given me, for they are yours; [10]all mine are yours, and yours are mine, and I am glorified in them. [11]And now I am no more in the world, but they are in the world, and I am coming to you. Holy Father, keep them in your name, which you have given me, that they may be one, even as we are one. [12]While I was with them, I kept them in your name, which you have given me; I have guarded them, and none of them is lost but the son of perdition, that the Scripture might be fulfilled. [13]But now I am coming to you; and these things I speak in the world, that they may have my joy fulfilled in themselves. [14]I have given them your word; and the world has hated them because they are not of the world, even as I am not of the world. [15]I do not pray that you should take them out of the world, but that you should keep them from the evil one.[k] [16]They are not of the world, even as I am not of the world. [17]Sanctify them in the truth; your word is truth. [18]As you sent me into the world, so I have sent them into the world. [19]And for their sake I consecrate myself, that they also may be consecrated in truth.

20 "I do not pray for these only, but also for those who believe in me through their word, [21]that they may all be one; even as you, Father, are in me, and I in you, that they also may be in us, so that the world may believe that you have sent me. [22]The glory which you have given me I have given to them, that they may be one even as we are one, [23]I in them and you in me, that they may become perfectly one, so that the world may know that you have sent me and have loved them even as you have loved me. [24]Father, I desire that they also, whom you have given me, may be with me where I am, to behold my glory which you have given me in your love for me before the foundation of the world. [25]O righteous Father, the world has not known you, but I have known you; and these know that you have sent me. [26]I made known to them your name, and I will make it known, that the love with which you have loved me may be in them, and I in them."

The Arrest of Jesus

18 When Jesus had spoken these words, he went forth with his disciples across the Kidron valley, where there was a garden, which he and his disciples entered. [2]Now Judas, who betrayed him, also knew the place; for Jesus often met there with his disciples. [3]So Judas, procuring a band of soldiers and some officers from the chief priests and the Pharisees, went there with lanterns and torches and weapons. [4]Then Jesus, knowing all that was to befall him, came forward and said to them, "Whom do you seek?" [5]They answered him, "Jesus of Nazareth." Jesus said to them, "I am he." Judas, who

---

17:9: Lk 22:32; Jn 14:16.   **17:11:** Phil 2:9; Rev 19:12; Rom 12:5; Gal 3:28; Jn 17:21.   **17:12:** Ps 41:9; Jn 6:70; 18:9.
17:14: Jn 15:19; 8:23.   **17:21:** Jn 10:38; 17:11.   **17:24:** Jn 1:14; 17:5; Mt 25:34.
18:1: Mt 26:30, 36; Mk 14:26, 32; Lk 22:39; Jn 17:23.   **18:3-11:** Mt 26:47-56; Mk 14:43-50; Lk 22:47-53.
18:4: Jn 6:64; 13:1.

---

ancient belief, held dear both in Israel and in the Church, stands in sharp contrast to the pagan notion that many gods exist and deserve our recognition (Ex 20:3-6; Is 43:10; 1 Cor 8:5-6).

17:6 manifested your name: Possibly the divine name "I AM", which is shared by Jesus (8:58; 18:6). Or, too, it may refer to the general revelation of the Father's life and love through the Incarnation (14:6-11) (CCC 2812). See note on 6:20.

17:11 as we are one: The family unity of the apostles is to reflect the family oneness of the Divine Persons in the Trinity (10:30).

17:12 the son of perdition: Judas Iscariot, whose betrayal of the Messiah was foretold in passages such as Ps 41:9 (13:18) and Ps 69:25 (Acts 1:20). See note on Mt 26:56.

17:14 not of the world: The disciples remain *in* the world after Jesus returns to the Father, but they are not *of* the world, because they are not allied with the godless forces that fight against the kingdom of God (15:18-24). See note on 1:10.

17:15 from the evil one: The prayer of Jesus becomes our prayer every time we utter the Our Father (Mt 6:13; CCC 2850-54).

17:17 Sanctify them: To "sanctify" means to consecrate for a holy purpose, which here concerns the spread and preservation of divine truth. The task of the apostles is to speak the **word** of the Lord both orally (1 Thess 2:13; 1 Pet 1:25) and in writing (2 Thess 2:15; 1 Tim 3:14-15). • Similar language is used in the OT for the consecration and ordination of Aaronic

priests (Ex 29:1; 40:12-13). Here the disciples are set apart for "the priestly service of the gospel" (Rom 15:16) (CCC 611).

17:18 so I have sent them: The mission of Christ becomes the mission of the Church once he returns to the Father. Although cooperation in this work is incumbent upon all baptized believers (CCC 1268-70), the apostles are sent forth in a special way for the ministry of preaching the word and sanctifying the world. This missionary mandate continues to be fulfilled by the bishops, who are the ordained successors to apostles (1 Tim 4:13-16; 2 Tim 2:1-2) (CCC 858-62).

17:20 those who believe: Jesus' prayer reaches into the future to bless believers of every age (20:29).

17:23 that the world may know: Envisions unity that is not only spiritual, but also visible and organizational, so that even the world can see it clearly (Eph 4:4-13). The indivisible unity of the Trinity is the source and pattern of this ecclesial oneness (17:11, 21-22). See note on 10:16.

17:24 may be with me: A prayer for the salvation of believers (14:2-3).

18:1 the Kidron valley: The deep ravine directly east of Jerusalem, separating the city from the Mount of Olives. The garden area on the western slope of the mount is called "Gethsemane" (Mt 26:36).

18:3 band of soldiers: A detachment (cohort) of several hundred Roman troops accompanied by Temple policemen (Acts 5:24-26). The authorities must have anticipated resistance from Jesus and his followers as they came armed in such large numbers.

---

[k] Or *from evil.*

betrayed him, was standing with them. [6]When he said to them, "I am he," they drew back and fell to the ground. [7]Again he asked them, "Whom do you seek?" And they said, "Jesus of Nazareth." [8]Jesus answered, "I told you that I am he; so, if you seek me, let these men go." [9]This was to fulfil the word which he had spoken, "Of those whom you gave me I lost not one." [10]Then Simon Peter, having a sword, drew it and struck the high priest's slave and cut off his right ear. The slave's name was Malchus. [11]Jesus said to Peter, "Put your sword into its sheath; shall I not drink the chalice which the Father has given me?"

Jesus before the High Priest

12 So the band of soldiers and their captain and the officers of the Jews seized Jesus and bound him. [13]First they led him to Annas; for he was the father-in-law of Cai′aphas, who was high priest that year. [14]It was Cai′aphas who had given counsel to the Jews that it was expedient that one man should die for the people.

Peter Denies Jesus

15 Simon Peter followed Jesus, and so did another disciple. As this disciple was known to the high priest, he entered the court of the high priest along with Jesus, [16]while Peter stood outside at the door. So the other disciple, who was known to the high priest, went out and spoke to the maid who kept the door, and brought Peter in. [17]The maid who kept the door said to Peter, "Are not you also one of this man's disciples?" He said, "I am not." [18]Now the servants[f] and officers had made a charcoal fire, because it was cold, and they were stand-ing and warming themselves; Peter also was with them, standing and warming himself.

The High Priest Questions Jesus

19 The high priest then questioned Jesus about his disciples and his teaching. [20]Jesus answered him, "I have spoken openly to the world; I have always taught in synagogues and in the temple, where all Jews come together; I have said nothing secretly. [21]Why do you ask me? Ask those who have heard me, what I said to them; they know what I said." [22]When he had said this, one of the officers standing by struck Jesus with his hand, saying, "Is that how you answer the high priest?" [23]Jesus answered him, "If I have spoken wrongly, bear witness to the wrong; but if I have spoken rightly, why do you strike me?" [24]Annas then sent him bound to Cai′aphas the high priest.

Peter Denies Jesus Again

25 Now Simon Peter was standing and warming himself. They said to him, "Are not you also one of his disciples?" He denied it and said, "I am not." [26]One of the servants[f] of the high priest, a kinsman of the man whose ear Peter had cut off, asked, "Did I not see you in the garden with him?" [27]Peter again denied it; and at once the cock crowed.

Jesus before Pilate

28 Then they led Jesus from the house of Cai′aphas to the praetorium. It was early. They themselves did not enter the praetorium, so that they might not be defiled, but might eat the Passover. [29]So Pilate went out to them and said, "What accusation do you bring against this man?" [30]They answered him, "If this man were not an evildoer,

---

18:9: Jn 17:12; 6:39. **18:11:** Mk 10:38; 14:36. **18:12-13:** Mt 26:57; Mk 14:53; Lk 22:54; 3:2. **18:14:** Jn 11:49-51. **18:15-16:** Mt 26:58; Mk 14:54; Lk 22:54. **18:17-18:** Mt 26:69-72; Mk 14:66-69; Lk 22:56-58. **18:19-23:** Mt 26:59-66; Mk 14:55-64; Lk 22:67-71. **18:23:** Mt 5:39; Acts 23:2-5. **18:24:** Jn 18:13; Lk 3:2. **18:25-27:** Mt 26:73-75; Mk 14:70-72; Lk 22:59-62. **18:28:** Jn 11:55; Mt 27:1-2; Mk 15:1; Lk 23:1. **18:29-38:** Mt 27:11-14; Mk 15:2-5; Lk 23:2-3.

18:6 I am: Jesus unleashes the power of the divine name, "I AM", simply by uttering it (Ex 3:14). See note on 6:20.

18:10 a sword: Peter's zeal unsheathes the weapon in defense of Jesus. Here and elsewhere he fails to understand how the betrayal and suffering of Christ are part of the Father's plan (Mt 16:21-23). Luke notes how Jesus rectifies his wrong by healing the slave's ear (Lk 22:51).

18:11 the chalice: The chalice of suffering that Jesus will drink on the Cross (Mk 10:38; CCC 607). See note on Lk 22:17.

18:13 Annas: The high priest of Israel from A.D. 6 to 15. Because the Romans deposed and replaced him with another priest contrary to the regulations of the Torah, many Jews still revered him as the rightful head of Israel even after he was relieved of his duties (18:19; Acts 4:6). **Caiaphas:** The son-in-law of Annas and the officiating high priest from A.D. 18 to 36.

18:14 one man should die: A reminder of the prophecy in 11:47-53. See note on 11:51.

18:15 another disciple: Probably John the evangelist, who never reveals his name in the Gospel but calls himself the disciple "whom Jesus loved" (13:23; 19:26; 20:2; 21:7). One tradition preserved by Eusebius holds that the Apostle John was born of a Jewish priestly family, which could explain his famil-iarity with the high priest (18:15), the name of the high priest's slave (18:10), and the family of the slave (18:26). See introduction: *Author.*

18:24 bound to Caiaphas: John summarizes Jesus' night-time trial before the Sanhedrin in this one statement (Mt 26:57-68; Mk 14:53-65). He gives greater attention to Jesus' interrogation before Pilate (18:33-38).

18:27 again denied it: Three times Peter denies his association with Jesus (18:17, 25), just as three times he fell asleep while Jesus prayed in agony (Mk 14:32-42) and three times he will renew his commitment to Jesus after the Resurrection (21:15-17). **the cock crowed:** Possibly the Roman bugle call that signaled the end of the "cockcrow" at about 3 A.M. See note on Mk 13:35.

18:28 the praetorium: The official residence of the Roman governor in Jerusalem. It served as his headquarters during Israel's annual feasts and other occasions that required his presence to maintain civil order in the city. **It was early:** On the morning of Good Friday. **did not enter:** Jews generally declined to enter the home of a Gentile for fear of ritual defilement (Acts 10:28). This was all the more important at Passover, since defilement automatically disqualified Jews from celebrating the feast for an entire month (Num 9:6-11).

18:29 Pilate: The Roman governor of Judea from A.D. 26 to 36. See note on Mt 27:2.

---

[f] Or *slaves.*

we would not have handed him over." ³¹Pilate said to them, "Take him yourselves and judge him by your own law." The Jews said to him, "It is not lawful for us to put any man to death." ³²This was to fulfil the word which Jesus had spoken to show by what death he was to die.

Jesus Sentenced to Death

33 Pilate entered the praetorium again and called Jesus, and said to him, "Are you the King of the Jews?" ³⁴Jesus answered, "Do you say this of your own accord, or did others say it to you about me?" ³⁵Pilate answered, "Am I a Jew? Your own nation and the chief priests have handed you over to me; what have you done?" ³⁶Jesus answered, "My kingship is not of this world; if my kingship were of this world, my servants would fight, that I might not be handed over to the Jews; but my kingship is not from the world." ³⁷Pilate said to him, "So you are a king?" Jesus answered, "You say that I am a king. For this I was born, and for this I have come into the world, to bear witness to the truth. Every one who is of the truth hears my voice." ³⁸Pilate said to him, "What is truth?"

After he had said this, he went out to the Jews again, and told them, "I find no crime in him. ³⁹But you have a custom that I should release one man for you at the Passover; will you have me release for you the King of the Jews?" ⁴⁰They cried out again, "Not this man, but Barab′bas!" Now Barabbas was a robber.

19 Then Pilate took Jesus and scourged him. ²And the soldiers plaited a crown of thorns, and put it on his head, and clothed him in a purple robe; ³they came up to him, saying, "Hail, King of the Jews!" and struck him with their hands. ⁴Pilate

---

18:32: Jn 3:14; 12:32.   **18:36:** Jn 6:15; Mt 26:53.   **18:37:** Jn 3:32; 8:14, 47; 1 Jn 4:6.
18:38–40: Mt 27:15–26; Mk 15:6–15; Lk 23:18–19; Acts 3:14.
19:2–3: Mt 27:27–31; Mk 15:16–20; Lk 22:63–65; 23:11.   **19:4:** Jn 18:38; 19:6; Lk 23:4.

18:31 It is not lawful: The Romans denied the authorities of Israel the right to administer capital punishment. Only the Romans themselves could put a condemned criminal to death, either by beheading (Roman citizens) or by crucifixion (non-citizens and insurrectionists). That Jesus was a Jewish peasant charged with sedition made crucifixion inevitable (CCC 596).
18:32 what death: Jesus was alluding to crucifixion when he spoke of being "lifted up" (3:14; 12:32).
18:33 King of the Jews?: The accusation of Jesus' enemies (Lk 23:2). The title functions as a slogan that is meant to resonate with Pilate as a threat to Roman rule (19:12).
18:36 My kingship: Jesus does not deny his royal mission, but he disassociates it from the political form of government that concerns Pilate. He thus turns the focus toward heaven, where he will be crowned not with gold but with glory and honor (Heb 2:9) and where homage is paid to him not in taxes but in worship (9:38) and allegiance to the truth (8:31–32). The coronation of Jesus begins with his Passion and culminates with his Ascension (Eph 1:20–23), from which time his domin-ion extends over the earth through the preaching and sacramental ministry of the Church (Mt 28:18–20).
18:38 What is truth?: The cynical response shows Pilate to be politically disinterested in the otherworldly perspective of Jesus. The irony here is that, while Pilate sees "truth" as a harmless abstraction, the acceptance of the gospel throughout the Roman world will eventually lead to the downfall of the Empire and the rise of a Christian civilization in its place (CCC 2471).
18:40 a robber: Or "revolutionary". Elsewhere Barabbas is described as an insurrectionist and a murderer (Mk 15:7).
19:1 scourged: Flogging was a cruel prelude to crucifixion in Roman practice. Tied to the ends of the whip were fragments of bone or metal designed to tear up the skin, causing injuries that were sometimes fatal. Pilate may have ordered this measure to appease the Jews, since he already felt there were no legal grounds to execute Jesus (18:38).
19:2–3 The royal tribute of the soldiers is both an act of mockery and an ironic witness to the kingship of Jesus (1:49; 18:36).

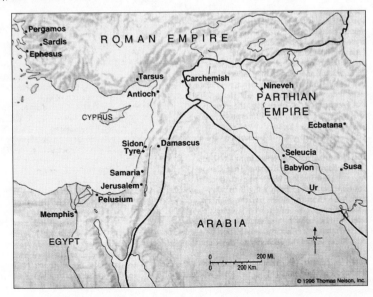

Roman Control
of Palestine
at the Time
of Christ

went out again, and said to them, "Behold, I am bringing him out to you, that you may know that I find no crime in him." [5]So Jesus came out, wearing the crown of thorns and the purple robe. Pilate said to them, "Here is the man!" [6]When the chief priests and the officers saw him, they cried out, "Crucify him, crucify him!" Pilate said to them, "Take him yourselves and crucify him, for I find no crime in him." [7]The Jews answered him, "We have a law, and by that law he ought to die, because he has made himself the Son of God." [8]When Pilate heard these words, he was even more afraid; [9]he entered the praetorium again and said to Jesus, "Where are you from?" But Jesus gave no answer. [10]Pilate therefore said to him, "You will not speak to me? Do you not know that I have power to release you, and power to crucify you?" [11]Jesus answered him, "You would have no power over me unless it had been given you from above; therefore he who delivered me to you has the greater sin."

12 Upon this Pilate sought to release him, but the Jews cried out, "If you release this man, you are not Caesar's friend; every one who makes himself a king sets himself against Caesar." [13]When Pilate heard these words, he brought Jesus out and sat down on the judgment seat at a place called The Pavement, and in Hebrew, Gab'batha. [14]Now it was the day of Preparation of the Passover; it was about the sixth hour. He said to the Jews, "Here is your King!" [15]They cried out, "Away with him, away with him, crucify him!" Pilate said to them, "Shall I crucify your King?" The chief priests answered, "We have no king but Caesar." [16]Then he handed him over to them to be crucified.

The Crucifixion

17 So they took Jesus, and he went out, bearing his own cross, to the place called the place of a skull, which is called in Hebrew Gol'gotha. [18]There they crucified him, and with him two others, one on either side, and Jesus between them. [19]Pilate also wrote a title and put it on the cross; it read, "Jesus of Nazareth, the King of the Jews." [20]Many of the Jews read this title, for the place where Jesus was crucified was near the city; and it was written in Hebrew, in Latin, and in Greek. [21]The chief priests of the Jews then said to Pilate, "Do not write, 'The King of the Jews,' but, 'This man said, I am King of the Jews.'" [22]Pilate answered, "What I have written I have written."

23 When the soldiers had crucified Jesus they took his garments and made four parts, one for each soldier; also his tunic. But the tunic was without seam, woven from top to bottom; [24]so they said to one another, "Let us not tear it, but cast lots for it

---

19:7: Lev 24:16; Mk 14:61–64; Jn 5:18; 10:33.   **19:11:** Rom 13:1; Jn 18:28.   **19:12:** Lk 23:2.
19:14: Mk 15:42; Jn 19:31, 42; Mk 15:25, 33.   **19:17–24:** Mt 27:33–44; Mk 15:22–32; Lk 33:33–43.
19:24: Ex 28:32; Ps 22:18.

19:6 Crucify him: The Jerusalem authorities incite a chanting mob in order to crush remaining sympathies for Jesus and bend the will of Pilate in the direction of their own (CCC 597, 600). I **find no crime:** The third time Pilate acquits Jesus of the charges laid against him (18:38; 19:4). Luke's trial narrative likewise stresses the innocence of Jesus (Lk 23:4, 15, 22, 41, 47).

19:7 he ought to die: A charge of blasphemy, which was a capital crime in the civil law of ancient Israel (Lev 24:16). Similar accusations are made at 5:18 and 10:33.

19:11 no power over me: Jesus, not Pilate, controls the situation, and so death cannot be forced upon him unwillingly (10:18). **from above:** Authority over the temporal affairs of society is granted to civil officials by God, not by governments themselves or by the consent of those they govern (Rom 13:1). **the greater sin:** Implies that Pilate shares the blame for Jesus' death, even though Judas and the Jerusalem leaders are even more culpable (Acts 4:27).

19:12 not Caesar's friend: An attempt to blackmail Pilate, who could face charges of disloyalty to the emperor if he lets a (supposed) royal claimant like Jesus go unpunished.

19:13 The Pavement: A stone slab platform. The Semitic expression **Gabbatha** refers to some sort of elevation.

19:14 day of Preparation: The day of Passover coincided with the Sabbath day in the year that Jesus died (A.D. 30). Thus, what is here called the day of Preparation for Passover is called the day of Preparation for the Sabbath in 19:31. **the sixth hour:** About noon, when lambs were being slain in the Temple courts for the Passover meal that night. The condemnation and death of Jesus at this time makes the point that he is the true Pascal Lamb, whose sacrifice is made in preparation for the eucharistic meal of the New Covenant (1:29; 1 Cor 5:7–8) (CCC 613–14).

19:15 no king but Caesar: A compromise so extreme that the Jerusalem authorities deny even the kingship of Yahweh (1 Sam 8:7).

19:17 bearing his own cross: Refers to the wooden cross-beam to be fixed horizontally to an upright stake at the execution site. See note on Mk 15:24.

19:18 one on either side: The four Gospels agree that Jesus was crucified between two criminals (Mt 27:38; Mk 15:27; Lk 23:33). • John's description is similar to that in the Greek version of Ex 17:12, where Moses' arms were suspended in the air by Aaron and Hur as they stood on either side of him. This was to ensure for Israel a military victory over the Amalekites. Jesus' arms are similarly stretched out between two men as he triumphs over the unseen armies of the devil (Col 2:14–15).

19:20 this title: Signs were hung around the necks of crucified victims and then fastened to their crosses. Listed on these placards was a brief inventory of the criminal charges brought against them. The trilingual inscription of Pilate could be read by everyone in the region: **Hebrew** was the religious language of Israel still known in parts of Judea; **Latin** was the official language of the Roman occupiers of Palestine; and **Greek** was the commercial language of the eastern Mediterranean world (CCC 440).

19:23 the tunic: A one-piece garment worn next to the skin. • The seamless tunic of Christ recalls the linen vestment worn by the high priest of Israel (Lev 16:4), which was not to be torn (Lev 21:10) and which, according to the historian Josephus, was seamless. This implies that Christ acts as a high priest when he makes himself a sacrifice on the Cross (Heb 2:17; 9:11–14). • Allegorically (St. Cyprian, *The Unity of the Catholic Church* 7), the seamless tunic signifies the indivisible kingdom of Christ. Although Solomon's kingdom was rent asunder like a garment and its glory passed away (1 Kings 11:29–32), the Church of Christ is forever glorious and will always remain intact (19:24).

19:24 They parted my garments: A quotation from Ps 22:18, a psalm that runs parallel to the entire plot of the Passion narrative. See note on Mt 27:46.

to see whose it shall be." This was to fulfil the Scripture,

"They parted my garments among them,
and for my clothing they cast lots."

25 So the soldiers did this. But standing by the cross of Jesus were his mother, and his mother's sister, Mary the wife of Clopas, and Mary Mag´dalene. ²⁶When Jesus saw his mother, and the disciple whom he loved standing near, he said to his mother, "Woman, behold, your son!" ²⁷Then he said to the disciple, "Behold, your mother!" And from that hour the disciple took her to his own home.

28 After this Jesus, knowing that all was now finished, said (to fulfil the Scripture), "I thirst." ²⁹A bowl full of vinegar stood there; so they put a sponge full of the vinegar on hyssop and held it to his mouth. ³⁰When Jesus had received the vinegar, he said, "It is finished"; and he bowed his head and gave up his spirit.

Jesus' Side Is Pierced

31 Since it was the day of Preparation, in order to prevent the bodies from remaining on the cross on the sabbath (for that sabbath was a high day), the Jews asked Pilate that their legs might be broken, and that they might be taken away. ³²So the soldiers came and broke the legs of the first, and of the other who had been crucified with him; ³³but when they came to Jesus and saw that he was already dead, they did not break his legs. ³⁴But one of the soldiers pierced his side with a spear, and at once there came out blood and water. ³⁵He who saw it has borne witness—his testimony is true, and he knows that he tells the truth—that you also may believe. ³⁶For these things took place that the Scripture might be fulfilled, "Not a bone of him shall be broken." ³⁷And again another Scripture says, "They shall look on him whom they have pierced."

The Burial of Jesus

38 After this Joseph of Arimathe´a, who was a disciple of Jesus, but secretly, for fear of the Jews, asked Pilate that he might take away the body of Jesus, and Pilate gave him leave. So he came and took away his body. ³⁹Nicode´mus also, who had at first come to him by night, came bringing a mixture of myrrh and aloes, about a hundred pounds' weight. ⁴⁰They took the body of Jesus, and bound it in linen cloths with the spices, as is the burial custom of the Jews. ⁴¹Now in the place where he was crucified there was a garden, and in the garden a new tomb where no one had ever been laid.

19:25: Mt 27:55–56; Mk 15:40–41; Lk 23:49; Jn 2:3; Mk 3:31; Lk 24:18; Jn 20:1, 18.   **19:26:** Jn 13:23; 20:2; 21:20.
19:28–30: Ps 69:21; Mt 27:45–50; Mk 15:33–37; Lk 23:44–46; Jn 17:4.   **19:31:** Deut 21:23; Ex 12:16.   **19:34:** 1 Jn 5:6–8.
19:35: Jn 15:27; 21:24.   **19:36:** Ex 12:46; Num 9:12; Ps 34:20.   **19:37:** Zech 12:10.
19:38–42: Mt 27:57–61; Mk 15:42–47; Lk 23:50–56.   **19:39:** Jn 3:1; 7:50.   **19:40:** Mk 16:1; 14:8.

19:25 his mother's sister: Possibly "Salome", the mother of the apostles James and John, the sons of Zebedee (Mt 27:56; Mk 15:40).

19:26 Woman: The address sounds impersonal to modern readers but was considered polite in biblical antiquity. ● Jesus probably alludes to Gen 3:15, which describes the mother of the Messiah as the "woman" whose offspring conquers the devil (CCC 726, 2618). See note on 2:4. **behold your son!:** Jesus honors his Mother by entrusting her to the protective care of the Apostle John, presumably because Mary had no other children to assume the responsibility. See note on Mt 12:46. ● John is not just an *individual* disciple, he is portrayed by the evangelist as an *icon* of every disciple whom Jesus loves. In this sense, Mary is given to all beloved disciples of Christ, just as every disciple is given to the maternal care of Mary. The assumption here is that family relations are extended beyond the limits of natural lineage, so that every baptized believer has God as a Father, Christ as an eldest brother, Mary as a Mother, and the saints as brothers and sisters (CCC 501, 964, 2679). See introduction: *Themes and Characteristics*.

19:28 I thirst: Recalls Ps 22:15 and Ps 69:21.

19:29 vinegar: Sour wine. This was not the narcotic drink that Jesus earlier refused (Mk 15:23). ● The use of **hyssop** to lift the sponge to Jesus suggests a connection with the original Passover, when the Israelites used hyssop branches to smear blood on their doorposts as a mark of divine protection (Ex 12:21–23).

19:32 broke the legs: A mallet was used to crush the leg bones and hasten the processes of death.

19:34 blood and water: Stresses the reality and finality of Jesus' death. ● The episode is reminiscent of Num 20:10–13 as read in Jewish tradition. In the original story only water issued from the rock struck by Moses, but in the Aramaic rendition both blood and water gushed forth (*Palestinian Targum* on Num 20:11). Paul similarly interprets this rock as a symbol of Christ, from which flows the spiritual drink of the Eucharist (1 Cor 10:4) and the Spirit (1 Cor 12:13). ● Allegorically (St. John Chrysostom, *Baptismal Instructions* 3, 16–19), the water and blood streaming from the side of Christ are symbolic of the new life we receive in Baptism (3:5) and the nourishment we receive in the Eucharist (6:53) (CCC 1225). It indicates, moreover, that the Church constituted by these sacraments is the bride of Christ that issues from his side, just as Eve came forth from the side of Adam (Gen 2:21–23). In another sense (Tertullian, *On Baptism* 16,2), the blood and water signify the two baptisms of martyrdom and Christian initiation.

19:35 he tells the truth: The evangelist verifies the historical facts of the Crucifixion as an eyewitness (19:26).

19:36 Not a bone: A reference to Ex 12:46. ● This restriction was part of Israel's Passover legislation that disqualified lambs with blemishes and broken bones from being slaughtered and eaten for the liturgical celebration (Ex 12:5; Num 9:11–12). Jesus, whose bones are left intact, is the unblemished Lamb (1:29) fit to be consumed in the eucharistic liturgy (6:53–58; CCC 608).

19:37 They shall look: A reference to Zech 12:10. ● Zechariah describes a day of mourning for Jerusalem, which will weep with remorse that its sins have pierced the Messiah. It is also a day of compassion, when Yahweh opens a fountain to cleanse the city of its iniquities (Zech 13:1). John may be suggesting, in light of the full context of this prophecy, that there is a close connection between the *piercing* of the Messiah and the *opening* of the fountain of divine mercy.

19:38 Joseph of Arimathea: A wealthy follower of Jesus who provided the tomb (Mt 27:57–60). He is a member of the Jewish Sanhedrin, although he did not consent to its condemnation of Christ (Lk 23:50–51; CCC 596).

19:39 Nicodemus: Also a member of the Sanhedrin (3:1).

19:40 the burial custom: For the procedure, see note on 11:17.

⁴²So because of the Jewish day of Preparation, as the tomb was close at hand, they laid Jesus there.

The Resurrection of Jesus

20 Now on the first day of the week, Mary Mag´dalene came to the tomb early, while it was still dark, and saw that the stone had been taken away from the tomb. ²So she ran, and went to Simon Peter and the other disciple, the one whom Jesus loved, and said to them, "They have taken the Lord out of the tomb, and we do not know where they have laid him." ³Peter then came out with the other disciple, and they went toward the tomb. ⁴They both ran, but the other disciple outran Peter and reached the tomb first; ⁵and stooping to look in, he saw the linen cloths lying there, but he did not go in. ⁶Then Simon Peter came, following him, and went into the tomb; he saw the linen cloths lying, ⁷and the napkin, which had been on his head, not lying with the linen cloths but rolled up in a place by itself. ⁸Then the other disciple, who reached the tomb first, also went in, and he saw and believed; ⁹for as yet they did not know the Scripture, that he must rise from the dead. ¹⁰Then the disciples went back to their homes.

Jesus Appears to Mary Magdalene

11 But Mary stood weeping outside the tomb, and as she wept she stooped to look into the tomb; ¹²and she saw two angels in white, sitting where the body of Jesus had lain, one at the head and one at the feet. ¹³They said to her, "Woman, why are you weeping?" She said to them, "Because they have taken away my Lord, and I do not know where they have laid him." ¹⁴Saying this, she turned round and saw Jesus standing, but she did not know that it was Jesus. ¹⁵Jesus said to her, "Woman, why are you weeping? Whom do you seek?" Supposing him to be the gardener, she said to him, "Sir, if you have carried him away, tell me where you have laid him, and I will take him away." ¹⁶Jesus said to her, "Mary." She turned and said to him in Hebrew, "Rab-bo´ni!" (which means Teacher). ¹⁷Jesus said to her, "Do not hold me, for I have not yet ascended to the Father; but go to my brethren and say to them, I am ascending to my Father and your Father, to my God and your God." ¹⁸Mary Mag´dalene went and said to the disciples, "I have seen the Lord"; and she told them that he had said these things to her.

Jesus Gives the Disciples the Power to Forgive Sins

19 On the evening of that day, the first day of the week, the doors being shut where the disciples were, for fear of the Jews, Jesus came and stood among them and said to them, "Peace be with you." ²⁰When he had said this, he showed them his hands and his side. Then the disciples were glad when they saw the Lord. ²¹Jesus said to them again, "Peace be with you. As the Father has sent me, even so I send you." ²²And when he had said this,

---

20:1-10: Mt 28:1-8; Mk 16:1-8; Lk 24:1-10. **20:3-10:** Lk 24:11-12. **20:9:** Lk 24:26, 46.
20:12: Lk 24:4; Mt 28:5; Mk 16:5. **20:13:** Jn 20:2. **20:14:** Mt 28:9; Jn 21:4. **20:17:** Jn 20:27; Mt 28:10; Jn 7:33.
20:18: Lk 24:10, 23. **20:19-20:** Lk 24:36-39. **20:21:** Jn 17:18; Mt 28:19. **20:22:** Acts 2:4, 33.

19:42 day of Preparation: The Sabbath is fast approaching (sundown Friday). By then labor must cease (Lk 23:56), and so corpses must be quickly buried (Deut 21:22-23).

20:1 the first day: Sunday, the first day of the Jewish week. **Mary Magdalene:** A devoted disciple of Christ, who was delivered of demonic possession (Lk 8:2) and whose love for Jesus carried her all the way to the Cross (19:25; CCC 641).

20:2 out of the tomb: The empty tomb is the indisputable fact of Easter morning, as testified to even by the Roman soldiers who guarded the site (Mt 28:11-15). The disappearance of Jesus is the first indication that he has risen as he said (Mt 20:17-19). This is confirmed by several appearances throughout the next 40 days (20:19-21; Acts 1:3; CCC 640). **we do not know:** Presumes that Mary has come to the tomb with other women, as in Mt 28:1, Mk 16:1, and Lk 23:55—24:1.

20:4 the other disciple: John, the evangelist himself. Luke makes similar mention of certain disciples, including Peter, running to the tomb on Easter morning (Lk 24:12, 24). See introduction: *Author*. **reached the tomb first:** John defers to Peter by letting him enter the tomb first (20:6). This is more than a polite gesture, as it reflects his deference to the preeminent honor and authority that Jesus has bestowed on Simon (Mt 16:16-19). • *Allegorically* (John Scotus Erigena, *Hom. in Prol. Jn.*), the tomb is the Sacred Scriptures. Peter is faith, which is the first thing we bring to its pages, and John is understanding, which afterward enters and penetrates their meaning more deeply. *Morally*, Peter and John represent the active and contemplative missions of the Church, so that even when contemplatives are the first to arrive at a deeper understanding of the faith, deference is given to the hierarchical leadership, who later defines and promulgates their authentic insights.

20:7 the napkin . . . the linen cloths: Corroborating evidence of the Resurrection. No thief would have taken the time to unwrap Jesus' corpse and fold his burial clothes neatly in the tomb. In any case, the grave robbers of antiquity usually stole the expensive linens and left the body behind, not the other way around.

20:9 the Scripture: For important resurrection passages, see note on Lk 24:46.

20:12 two angels: Luke likewise mentions two angels (Lk 24:4, 23).

20:14 she did not know: Failure to recognize the risen Jesus immediately is also noted in 21:4 and Lk 24:16 (CCC 659).

20:17 Do not hold me: Mary wants to keep Jesus with her, but he must first ascend to the Father. Only then will he come again to his disciples in spiritual and sacramental ways. See note on 14:18. **my Father and your Father:** Jesus is the Son of God by nature (1:18); believers are sons and daughters by grace (1:12); and all have the same Father (CCC 443, 654).

20:19 that day: The evening of Easter Sunday.

20:20 his hands and his side: The point is that Jesus is raised not simply with a body, but with the *same* body that was crucified and died only days earlier (20:25, 27). He carries these marks of his earthly sacrifice with him even when he ascends into heaven (Rev 5:6) (CCC 645).

20:21 Peace: A traditional Hebrew greeting. See note on 14:27.

20:22 he breathed on them: Anticipates the coming of the Spirit on Pentecost, which will take place 50 days later (Acts 2:1-4). Here we see that the risen humanity of Jesus has become a sacrament of the divine Spirit (6:53-58; CCC 1116). • John uses an expression that recurs in significant

he breathed on them, and said to them, "Receive the Holy Spirit. ²³If you forgive the sins of any, they are forgiven; if you retain the sins of any, they are retained."

Jesus and Thomas

24 Now Thomas, one of the Twelve, called the Twin, was not with them when Jesus came. ²⁵So the other disciples told him, "We have seen the Lord." But he said to them, "Unless I see in his hands the print of the nails, and place my finger in the mark of the nails, and place my hand in his side, I will not believe."

26 Eight days later, his disciples were again in the house, and Thomas was with them. The doors were shut, but Jesus came and stood among them, and said, "Peace be with you." ²⁷Then he said to Thomas, "Put your finger here, and see my hands; and put out your hand, and place it in my side; do not be faithless, but believing." ²⁸Thomas answered him, "My Lord and my God!" ²⁹Jesus said to him, "You have believed because you have seen me. Blessed are those who have not seen and yet believe."

The Purpose of This Book

30 Now Jesus did many other signs in the presence of the disciples, which are not written in this book; ³¹but these are written that you may believe that Jesus is the Christ, the Son of God, and that believing you may have life in his name.

Jesus Appears to Disciples by the Sea of Tiberias

21 After this Jesus revealed himself again to the disciples by the Sea of Tibe´ri-as; and he

revealed himself in this way. ²Simon Peter, Thomas called the Twin, Nathan´a-el of Cana in Galilee, the sons of Zeb´edee, and two others of his disciples were together. ³Simon Peter said to them, "I am going fishing." They said to him, "We will go with you." They went out and got into the boat; but that night they caught nothing.

4 Just as day was breaking, Jesus stood on the beach; yet the disciples did not know that it was Jesus. ⁵Jesus said to them, "Children, have you any fish?" They answered him, "No." ⁶He said to them, "Cast the net on the right side of the boat, and you will find some." So they cast it, and now they were not able to haul it in, for the quantity of fish. ⁷That disciple whom Jesus loved said to Peter, "It is the Lord!" When Simon Peter heard that it was the Lord, he put on his clothes, for he was stripped for work, and sprang into the sea. ⁸But the other disciples came in the boat, dragging the net full of fish, for they were not far from the land, but about a hundred yards *ᵐ* off.

9 When they got out on land, they saw a charcoal fire there, with fish lying on it, and bread. ¹⁰Jesus said to them, "Bring some of the fish that you have just caught." ¹¹So Simon Peter went aboard and hauled the net ashore, full of large fish, a hundred and fifty-three of them; and although there were so many, the net was not torn. ¹²Jesus said to them, "Come and have breakfast." Now none of the disciples dared ask him, "Who are you?" They knew it was the Lord. ¹³Jesus came and took the bread and gave it to them, and so with the fish. ¹⁴This was

---

20:23: Mt 16:19; 18:18.   **20:24:** Jn 11:16.   **20:27:** Lk 24:40.   **20:29:** 1 Pet 1:8.   **20:30:** Jn 21:25.
20:31: Jn 3:15.   **21:2:** Jn 11:16; 1:45; Lk 5:10.   **21:3–6:** Lk 5:3–7.   **21:4:** Jn 20:14; Lk 24:16.
21:5: Lk 24:41.   **21:7:** Jn 13:23; 19:26; 20:2; 21:20.

---

contexts in the Greek OT. It appears in Gen 2:7, where the Lord breathes life into Adam; in 1 Kings 17:21, where the Greek version specifies that Elijah resuscitated a boy with his breath; and in Ezek 37:9, where God raises an army of corpses to new life by the breath of the Spirit.

20:23 forgive the sins: Jesus' ministry of mercy and reconciliation will continue through the apostles (2 Cor 5:18–20; Jas 5:14–15). The power to "forgive and retain" sins in the name of Jesus is elsewhere described as the authority to "bind and loose" (Mt 16:19; 18:18; CCC 553, 730). • The Council of Trent connects this episode with the institution of the Sacrament of Reconciliation (Sess. 14, chap. 1), by which Christ distributes divine forgiveness to the world through the successors of the apostles (bishops) and their assistants in the presbyterate (priests) (CCC 976, 1441, 1461).

20:26 Eight days later: The second Sunday of the Easter octave.

20:28 My Lord and my God!: The climactic confession of faith in John's Gospel (CCC 448, 644).

20:30–31 A statement of purpose by the evangelist. He has written the Fourth Gospel both as history and as witness, in the hope that a factual portrayal of the Christ's life will not just inform readers, but challenge them to accept him and his claims with true faith (Lk 1:1–4).

21:1 Sea of Tiberias: Another name for the Sea of Galilee. See note on 6:1.

21:2 At least five of these seven disciples are apostles. John, who is one of the **sons of Zebedee** (Mt 10:2), remains consistent until the end in withholding his name from the Gospel narrative. See introduction: *Author* and chart: *The Twelve Apostles* at Mk 3.

21:3 that night: Net fishing was done at night (Lk 5:5). The most popular fish were tilapias, now called "Peter's fish".

21:7 It is the Lord!: John is the first to recognize Jesus on the shore. It is unclear whether his identity was veiled because of the distance, the lingering darkness, or a dullness of spiritual insight (20:14, Lk 24:16; CCC 645). • *Allegorically* (St. Gregory the Great, *Hom. in Evan.* 24), the presence of Christ on land signifies the stability and peace of his Resurrection life, as distinct from the instability and commotion of mortal life still experienced by the disciples as they labor upon the waves of the sea.

21:9 charcoal fire: This expression, used only here and in 18:18 in the NT, sets up the following conversation between Jesus and Peter. The point is that Peter is given a second chance to affirm his love for Christ in front of a fire after three times denying him in front of a fire (18:15–18, 25–27).

21:11 a hundred and fifty-three: The number of fish hauled ashore is symbolic. St. Jerome claims that Greek zoologists had identified 153 different kinds of fish (*Comm. in Ez.* 14, 47). If this is the background, the episode anticipates how the apostles, made fishers of men by Christ (Mt 4:19), will gather believers from every nation into the Church (Mt 28:18–20).

21:13 took . . . gave: The breakfast recalls the feeding of

ᵐ Greek *two hundred cubits.*

now the third time that Jesus was revealed to the disciples after he was raised from the dead.

Peter Is Given a Command

15 When they had finished breakfast, Jesus said to Simon Peter, "Simon, son of John, do you love me more than these?" He said to him, "Yes, Lord; you know that I love you." He said to him, "Feed my lambs." [16]A second time he said to him, "Simon, son of John, do you love me?" He said to him, "Yes, Lord; you know that I love you." He said to him, "Tend my sheep." [17]He said to him the third time, "Simon, son of John, do you love me?" Peter was grieved because he said to him the third time, "Do you love me?" And he said to him, "Lord, you know everything; you know that I love you." Jesus said to him, "Feed my sheep. [18]Truly, truly, I say to you, when you were young, you fastened your own belt and walked where you would; but when you are old, you will stretch out your hands, and another will fasten your belt for you and bring you where you do not wish to go." [19](This he said to show by

what death he was to glorify God.) And after this he said to him, "Follow me."

Jesus and the Beloved Disciple

20 Peter turned and saw following them the disciple whom Jesus loved, who had lain close to his breast at the supper and had said, "Lord, who is it that is going to betray you?" [21]When Peter saw him, he said to Jesus, "Lord, what about this man?" [22]Jesus said to him, "If it is my will that he remain until I come, what is that to you? Follow me!" [23]The saying spread abroad among the brethren that this disciple was not to die; yet Jesus did not say to him that he was not to die, but, "If it is my will that he remain until I come, what is that to you?"

24 This is the disciple who is bearing witness to these things, and who has written these things; and we know that his testimony is true.

25 But there are also many other things which Jesus did; were every one of them to be written, I suppose that the world itself could not contain the books that would be written.

21:14: Jn 20:19, 26.   **21:15:** Jn 1:42; 13:37; Mk 14:29–31; Lk 12:32.   **21:16:** Mt 2:6; Acts 20:28, 1 Pet 5:2; Rev 7:17.   **21:19:** 2 Pet 1:14; Mk 1:17.   **21:20:** Jn 13:25.   **21:22:** 1 Cor 4:5; Jas 5:7; Rev 2:25; Mt 16:28.   **21:24:** Jn 15:27; 19:35.   **21:25:** Jn 20:30.

---

the 5,000 in 6:1–14, since these are the only two meals in John eaten beside the Sea of Galilee and the only two where bread and fish are served. See note on 6:11.

21:14 the third time: i.e., that Jesus appears risen to the group of disciples. Individual encounters like the one in 20:16 are not included in this numbering.

21:15-17 Three times Peter reaffirms his love for Jesus as personal restitution for the three times he denied him (13:38; 18:15-18, 25-27). The dialogue in Greek makes use of several synonyms: two different nouns are used for *sheep*, and two different verbs are used for *feed, know,* and *love*. Although this may be a stylistic feature to avoid redundancy, others think it more significant, especially with the verb *love*. In his first two questions, Jesus asks Peter if he loves him with "willing love" (Gk. *agapaō*), but in the third question he asks if Peter loves him with merely "friendly affection" (Gk. *phileō*), which is the word Peter uses in all three of his responses. An intended distinction between these terms would indicate that Jesus, desirous of a complete and heroic love from Peter, was willing by the end of the conversation to settle for his friendship.

21:15 more than these?: Peter is challenged to live up to his own words, since earlier he declared that even if the other disciples should fall away from Christ, his commitment would never falter (Mt 26:33). **Feed my lambs:** Jesus entrusts

to Peter the task of shepherding his entire flock. This supreme leadership position over the Church gives him a unique share in the authority of Christ, who is still acknowledged by Peter as the "chief Shepherd" (1 Pet 5:4). It is important to recognize that no tension exists in the mind of Jesus between his own role as the "good shepherd" and the delegation of pastoral authority to Peter (10:11; CCC 553, 881). • Vatican I declared that in this episode Christ made Peter the visible head and chief pastor over the universal Church (*Pastor aeternus*, chap. 1). See note on Mt 16:13-20.

21:18 stretch out your hands: An allusion to Peter's martyrdom by crucifixion. Tradition holds that it took place in Rome around A.D. 67.

21:23 The saying spread: This verse is included to correct a misunderstanding among believers that the Apostle John would remain alive until Christ returns in glory.

21:24 This is the disciple: Equivalent to the evangelist's personal signature. See introduction: *Author*. **we know:** Apparently this comment was inserted, not by the evangelist, but by other Christians who knew the facts about Jesus as John did and willingly testified to the veracity of his Gospel.

21:25 many other things: John claims that his Gospel is accurate, not that it is comprehensive or exhaustive (19:35). He has given enough information about the life and ministry of Jesus to elicit faith from his readers (20:30-31; CCC 515).

STUDY QUESTIONS

Chapter 1

For understanding
1. **1:1.** How does John allude to the beginning of Genesis? Since Genesis states that God created the universe through a Word, what is John implying about it? What is the significance of John's saying that the Word "was God"?
2. **Word Study: Word.** With what did Greek philosophers associate the idea of the Word? What two traditions does the Bible associate with the idea of the Word? How does John seem to draw these strands together?
3. **1:14.** What is the connection between the Incarnation of God the Son and the erection, recounted in the Old Testament, of the Tabernacle in the wilderness? What does the expression "grace and truth" mean? How is that meaning linked to the idea of glory?
4. **1:49.** How is Nathanael's response to Jesus (who saw him under the fig tree) elicited by a knowledge of the Old Testament? What makes Nathanael think that he is standing before the Son of God?
5. **1:51.** How does Jesus place himself in the center of Jacob's dream of the ladder with angels ascending and descending? Why is this placement important to John's message?

For application
1. **1:12–13.** When did you first realize that you had become a child of God at Baptism? What kind of grace did this transformation take? How do you experience that grace in your daily life?
2. **1:18.** How is the Son making the Father known to you? How has your relationship with the Father changed as you have come to know the Son?
3. **1:29.** What does it mean to "behold" the Lamb of God? What are you supposed to see when you look at him? What kind of lamb takes away sin?
4. **1:38–39.** How has your curiosity about Jesus influenced your faith in him? In what circumstances have you heard Jesus' invitation to "come and see" where he lives?

Chapter 2

For understanding
1. **2:4.** How does Jesus' use of the word "woman" point to a parallel between Eve and Mary? In what two ways may the Hebrew idiom "what have you to do with me?" be understood? Which meaning best fits this context?
2. **2:10.** What associations might be attached to the steward's expression "the good wine" in this passage?
3. **Word Study: Signs.** Why does John call Jesus' miracles *signs*? What are the seven signs John reports in his Gospel?
4. **2:14–22.** In what two ways might one explain why John places the cleansing of the Temple at the beginning of Jesus' ministry, whereas the other Gospels place it near the end?

For application
1. **2:5.** How unconditionally do you do whatever Jesus tells you to do? Do you ever try to place limits on what he can tell you to do?
2. **2:15–16.** According to the textual note for this verse, Origen saw Jesus' action as driving out a lack of personal discipline and a herd of earthly attachments. What attachments do you have that Jesus might want to drive out of your heart (his Father's house)?
3. **2:17.** How does the verse from Psalm 69, quoted here, apply to you? How zealous are you for God's house? What forms does this zeal take?
4. **2:23–25.** What is the basis of your relationship with Jesus? How strong do you think it is? How reliable do you think he might find you?

Chapter 3

For understanding
1. **3:5.** What observations suggest that "water and the Spirit" refers to the Sacrament of Baptism? How did the Old Testament envision the link between water and the Spirit?
2. **3:14.** How does Jesus' reference to the bronze serpent in Numbers 21 refer to his own Crucifixion? What does the expression "be lifted up" mean?
3. **3:16.** What is the function of this verse in the text? How should the expression "eternal life" be understood in John? When does eternal life begin?
4. **3:36.** How is faith to be exercised? What is the connection between belief and obedience? If the opposite of faith is not merely unbelief, what is it?

For application
1. **3:8.** What experience in your own life shows a spontaneous action of the Holy Spirit that you did not recognize at the time (but did so later)? What caused you to think that it was the Spirit at work?
2. **3:11.** How have you testified to what you have seen of God's work? What forms has this testimony taken? How much of this testimony has been in words rather than in an overall way of life?
3. **3:30.** How does Jesus "increase" in your life? How do John's imperatives ("must increase . . . must decrease") apply to you?
4. **3:36.** What is the importance of obedience in this passage? What is your attitude to obedience when it comes to faith?

Chapter 4

For understanding
1. **4:10.** What two levels of meaning does the expression "living water" have? Look up Is 12:3, Ezek 47:1–12, and Zech 14:8. How do those passages use the idea of living water?
2. **4:18.** How does the woman's life with "five husbands" parallel the historical experience of the Samaritan people (see 2 Kings 17:24–31)? What does the name *Baal* mean?
3. **4:23.** What does the expression "in spirit and truth" mean?
4. **Topical Essay: The "Hour" of Jesus.** What function does the frequent mention of Jesus' "hour" have in John's Gospel? What are the two dimensions of this hour? Why are these two dimensions inseparable?

For application
1. **4:16–19.** Has the Spirit ever revealed something to you about yourself that you would just as soon have avoided knowing? What did you do about that revelation?
2. **4:28.** According to the note for this passage, what is the significance of the woman leaving her water jar by the well? As you discover the truth about Jesus, what does he want you to leave behind?
3. **4:34.** How can you regard doing God's will in your life as *food*? How are you nourished by doing his will?
4. **4:48–50.** How much does your faith rely on some kind of sign that God will do what he promises? Or how does it resemble that of the official who took Jesus at his word?

Chapter 5

For understanding
1. **5:5.** What about Israelite history might the 38-year duration of the man's illness recall?
2. **5:29.** When Christ claims the authority to raise both the righteous and the wicked from the dead, what two oracles from the Old Testament stand in the background of his claim? How does Jesus view himself in the light of these prophetic narratives?
3. **5:30-47.** Who or what are the witnesses Jesus calls on to verify the divine authority and mission given him from God? How many witnesses did Jewish legal tradition require to substantiate testimony?
4. **5:46.** What three passages from the Pentateuch substantiate Jesus' claim that Moses wrote of him?

For application
1. **5:6-9.** How does the paralyzed man answer Jesus' question about wanting to be well? When you pray, do you tend to ask for God's help confidently, or do you complain about your situation?
2. **5:14.** Jesus warns the man who has been cured not to sin any more now that he has been healed. What worse things might happen to the man if he sins now that he is well? What shape does your relationship with God take when you get sick? How does it change as you recover?
3. **5:30.** Jesus is the divine Son of the Father, yet whose will does he want to do? What happens when you try to do things your own way? How might you seek to imitate Jesus' attitude in your home or work life?
4. **5:39-40.** Jesus accuses his hearers of searching the Bible for eternal life but failing to see the witness Scripture gives to Jesus himself, who is the source of life. How often do you cling to prejudices and personal interpretations that make it difficult to hear what God is truly saying?

Chapter 6

For understanding
1. **6:4.** What happens during a Passover (seder) meal? Why does the evangelist mention the upcoming Passover feast?
2. **6:35-59.** What are two ways in which the Bread of Life discourse has been interpreted? How might the discourse be divided into two distinct parts? How do the two halves work together?
3. **6:53.** How do we know from this passage that Jesus is speaking literally and sacramentally, rather than metaphorically? Since the Old Testament forbids the drinking of blood, why does Jesus' injunction to drink his blood not fall under its prohibitions?
4. **Word Study: Eats (6:54).** What does *trōgō* actually mean in English? How does ancient Greek literature use the verb? Why does Jesus use such a graphic word instead of the normal vocabulary?

For application
1. **6:15-21.** What tends to happen in your life when you get impatient waiting for God to act and so start to take action yourself? What tends to happen when his help arrives (even if it appears to come late)?
2. **6:28-29.** What do you think Jesus means by saying that believing in him is doing God's work? Does believing mean assenting mentally to a theological position, or might it refer to something more active? If the latter, what?
3. **6:53-54.** How often do you go to Communion? What is your experience of God's life when you do? According to Jesus' promise in this passage, when does eternal life begin if you eat his flesh?
4. **6:60-65.** What are some of Jesus' "hard sayings" in the Gospels about living with God? How do they apply to you? Have you ever tried to get God to change his mind? What was the result?

Chapter 7

For understanding

1. **7:2.** What does the feast of Tabernacles (Booths) commemorate? What two liturgical ceremonies from this feast hang as a backdrop to Jesus' teaching in Jn 7—8?
2. **7:8.** When Jesus says that he is "not going up" to Jerusalem, what two levels of meaning does his expression have?
3. **7:27.** What two traditions regarding the birth and origin of the Messiah were in circulation in ancient Judaism? What irony is attached to these traditions?
4. **7:38.** What three Old Testament passages are summarized in John's statement that "out of his heart shall flow rivers of living water"? How do they point forward to Jesus?

For application

1. **7:16–18.** How careful are you to use discernment in the materials you read about Catholicism or in what you hear taught from the pulpit or in the classroom? If you have questions, what do you do about getting answers? If you teach others about the faith, how careful are you to ensure that you are teaching it accurately?
2. **7:24.** What does Jesus mean by judging here? How does he want you to judge? What should you be judging?
3. **7:37–39.** How do you recognize a thirst for Jesus in yourself? What do you do about it? How does Jesus want you to come to him to drink?
4. **7:40–52.** Most people have an opinion about who Jesus is and where he comes from. What is your own opinion at the moment? How has it changed over the years? How do you find out who Jesus really is?

Chapter 8

For understanding

1. **8:12.** What is the significance of the location where Jesus is standing as he calls himself the "light of the world"? What are three Old Testament themes that prepare the way for Jesus as the only "true light"?
2. **8:24.** Of what does Jesus stress the importance in the context of saying "I am he"? What Old Testament passage does this evoke?
3. **8:35.** In saying that the slave has no permanent residence in the household but that the son does, to what Old Testament story does Jesus allude? How does Jesus apply this narrative to the sons of Abraham of his own day?
4. **8:56.** When Jesus says that Abraham "rejoiced that he was to see my day", to what narrative in Genesis might this statement refer? In what ways?

For application

1. **8:11.** Though Jesus does not condemn the woman taken in adultery, what attitude does he take toward her sin? Compare this passage with Jn 5:14. What attitude should you take toward sin of any kind?
2. **8:31ff.** Why does Jesus seem deliberately to aggravate those who believe in him? On what are they relying? On what is he asking them to rely?
3. **8:31–32, 43–47.** Why is hearing the word of God difficult for people to bear? How easy is it for you to fool yourself (or be fooled) about yourself—and how hard is it for you to face the truth? When you face the truth, how does your relationship with God change?
4. **8:34–35.** How might you verify from experience that anyone who commits sin is a slave to it? If you continue to sin, how secure do you think your place is in God's household?

Chapter 9

For understanding
1. **9:2.** What have some people reading Scripture thought about the connection between sickness and sin? Whose sin? What does Jesus say about that connection?
2. **9:7.** What Old Testament episode does Jesus' command to the man born blind ("go, wash") recall? What is the pool of Siloam? Why does John make an editorial comment on the meaning of the name "Siloam"? Finally, how does this episode prepare for Baptism?
3. **9:11.** How does the perception of Jesus deepen as the story unfolds?
4. **9:39.** To whom does Jesus reveal or withhold revelation of the Father and his will? To what are the Pharisees blind?

For application
1. **9:19–23.** What are the blind man's parents afraid of? How do they deal with their fear? How have you responded when asked tough questions about your faith?
2. **9:24–34.** How does the blind man's character contrast with that of his parents? How willing are you to stand up for the facts against those who oppose you?
3. **9:35–37.** How does Jesus meet up with the blind man again? What does he ask of him? What does Jesus ask of you when you say that you "see" him?
4. **9:41.** How would you translate Jesus' remark in terms of your own life? Why would sin remain for those who claim to "see" but are blind? What is the sin that remains?

Chapter 10

For understanding
1. **10:11.** Although Yahweh was the divine Shepherd of Israel in the Old Testament, how did he exercise his rule? How will he exercise it in the last days?
2. **10:16.** To whom does the phrase "other sheep" refer? If there is one flock and one shepherd, where does the authority of Peter and the apostles come from? The Apostles' Creed enumerates the four marks of the Church; what does it mean by the mark of oneness?
3. **10:22.** What is the feast of Hanukkah, and what does it commemorate?
4. **10:35.** When Jesus says that "Scripture cannot be nullified", what are three implications of his statement?

For application
1. **10:7–9.** How many gates does the sheepfold have that Jesus is describing? Who (not what) is that gate? Who is the only gatekeeper? What does all of this say about all other religious positions that do not acknowledge Jesus' role?
2. **10:10.** Why has Jesus come to you? What does that mean for you?
3. **10:17–18.** Even though the authorities will arrest, try, and execute Jesus, who has ultimate control over his destiny? What kind of assurance can you derive from this?
4. **10:28.** If no one can take Jesus' sheep out of his hand, what power does the world or the devil have over you? How, then, can a sheep of his be lost?

Chapter 11

For understanding
1. **11:17.** Why is the fact that Lazarus has been dead for four days decisive in this story? How did Jews in New Testament times prepare the dead for burial? From an allegorical perspective, what are the four stages of spiritual death?
2. **11:24.** Where in the Old Testament is a belief in the resurrection supported? What do some of the passages cited in the note say about it?
3. **11:33.** What is a more literal translation of the word rendered "troubled" in this passage? What may have prompted Jesus' emotional reaction?
4. **11:48.** What is so ironic about the Sanhedrin's fear that the Romans would come? Why did they come?

For application
1. **11:5–6.** Having been told that Jesus loved Lazarus, Martha, and Mary, what do you make of the verse that begins, "So when he heard . . ."? How is his deliberate delay a sign of love? When Jesus delays answering your requests to come speedily, how do you interpret the delay?
2. **11:24–26.** What does Jesus mean by identifying resurrection and life with himself? When you think of your own death, what do you really believe about your resurrection? In that light, how do you regard your death?
3. **11:35.** Refer to the note for this verse. What are some of the other emotions that Jesus displays in the Gospels? How might an understanding of these reactions, and the events that prompted them, affect your faith in him?
4. **11:41–42a.** How does Jesus' prayer begin? How do your prayers begin? Faced with a difficult situation, how ready are you to acknowledge that God always hears you?

Chapter 12

For understanding
1. **12:8.** In the context of Deut 15:11, what point is Jesus making by saying that "the poor you always have with you, but you do not always have me"?
2. **12:15.** How does Jesus' entry into Jerusalem reflect the royal procession of the Messiah foretold by Zechariah? What was the point of riding on a donkey?
3. **12:32.** How does the expression "when I am lifted up" recall the fourth Servant Song from Isaiah? How does Jesus see himself as an embodiment of Isaiah's "ensign" posted for the gathering of the nations?
4. **12:40.** How do Isaiah's and Jesus' missions parallel each other?
5. **12:41.** How might the similar wording of Is 6:10 (alluded to in the preceding verse) and the Suffering Servant passage in Is 52:13 yield a new insight into the meaning of John's observation that Isaiah "saw his glory"?

For application
1. **12:3–5.** What does Judas' question imply about Mary's generosity? When have you criticized (or been criticized by) someone for being generous? What was the outcome of the criticism?
2. **12:24.** How has this principle of the spiritual life manifested itself in your life? How have you "died"? What was the fruit that resulted?
3. **12:27–28.** What is your response to intense personal suffering? How like Jesus' attitude is your own?
4. **12:42–43.** Have you ever been more concerned about the good opinion of others than about pleasing God? How does your desire for the respect of others influence the way you live your Catholic life?

Chapter 13

For understanding
1. **Topical Essay: When Did Jesus Celebrate the Last Supper?** From the archaeological, chronological, and traditional points of view, how does placing the Last Supper on Tuesday of Holy Week seem to give us a more coherent picture of Jesus' last days?
2. **13:4.** When Jesus lays aside his garments, what might this symbolize? How does the language of the verse make this clear?
3. **13:18.** Why does Jesus allude to Ps 41:9? How does the psalm end?
4. **13:34.** How does Jesus' new commandment of love go beyond that of the Old Covenant? Where does this love come from?

For application
1. **13:8.** Why would refusing to let Jesus minister to you mean that you had no part in him? How can you let him minister to you in your daily life?
2. **13:15-17.** If Jesus' words and actions are an example for you, why is it so hard to follow that example? In the context of Jesus' audience, what is the significance of the reference to servants and messengers? How do these words describe you?
3. **13:34-35.** How, according to Jesus, is his new commandment to be carried out? Would all know you are his disciple by the way *you* behave? Why or why not?
4. **13:37-38.** How committed to Jesus are you, really? How are you reminded of your weakness in that commitment?

Chapter 14

For understanding
1. **14:6.** What is Jesus claiming by calling himself "the way"? How many paths to heaven, then, are there?
2. **Word Study: Counselor.** In legal terms, what is a Paraclete? In what way is Jesus a Paraclete? How is the Holy Spirit a Paraclete?
3. **14:26.** Why is the third Person of the Trinity sent from heaven? What is Jesus promising by sending the Holy Spirit? What is he *not* promising?
4. **14:28.** When Jesus says that the Father is greater than he, what does he mean? If no one of the Divine Persons exceeds the others in greatness, how might you characterize the relation among them?

For application
1. **14:6.** What does Jesus' claim to be the "way, and the truth, and the life" mean for you personally? In what respects is Jesus the way for you? How is he the truth? How is he your life?
2. **14:15-17.** What does Jesus say is an indication of your love for him? According to the passage, how can you know that the Holy Spirit "dwells with you, and will be in you"?
3. **14:21-24.** In the context of all of these verses, what answer is Jesus giving to Judas' question? Why would Jesus manifest himself to the disciples but not to the world?
4. **14:25-27.** Is the peace Jesus offers a feeling or a relationship? In context, how is Jesus' peace different from that of the world? What is the relationship between peace and being troubled or afraid?

Chapter 15

For understanding
1. **15:1–11.** What does the metaphor of the vine assume, and who are the persons involved? When Jesus uses this Old Testament imagery, what is he stressing?
2. **15:6.** What fate awaits every branch that withers away from Christ? What other New Testament passages allude to this fate? How did Ezekiel use the same idea?
3. **15:14.** Why is the promise of intimacy with Jesus conditional? Who was the first person in the Bible to be called a "friend" of God?
4. **15:26.** What is the relationship of the Father and the Son in the sending of the Spirit? How does this passage support the wording in the Nicene Creed that the Spirit "proceeds from the Father and the Son"?

For application
1. **15:1–8.** What kind of "fruit" does the Father (the vinedresser) expect you to bear? When Jesus asserts that you can do nothing without him, what do you think he means? How literally do you think he means it?
2. **15:13.** How does Jesus lay down his life for his friends? How does he want you to lay down yours? What does he say is the measure of our love for one another (v. 12)?
3. **15:16.** Who does Jesus say initiates your relationship with him? What was the purpose of his choice?
4. **15:18–20.** Assuming the term "world" in this passage is not the physical creation, what is it? As a friend of Jesus, what can you expect from this "world"? Why?

Chapter 16

For understanding
1. **16:7.** How will it be to the disciples' advantage that Jesus go away from them? What benefits will the Spirit bring?
2. **16:8.** How does the Spirit "convince" the world of sin? In what juridical role does the Spirit act in this case?
3. **16:13.** In what way is the guiding mission of the Holy Spirit directly opposed to the work of Satan? How does this passage relate to the Second Vatican Council's teaching on infallibility?
4. **16:25.** To what is Jesus referring when he says he has been speaking in figures?

For application
1. **16:1–4a.** What strength does Jesus expect you to derive from his warning of future persecution? To which of the four cardinal virtues does his warning direct the mind (and therefore the will)?
2. **16:7–11.** What is the role of the Holy Spirit in your personal life?
3. **16:20–22.** Given the fact of Jesus' Resurrection, what is the joy that should be yours in your life with him? Why will no one be able to take that joy away from you?
4. **16:32–33.** What kinds of tribulation or suffering do you experience as coming from the world (not from the devil or yourself)? How does Jesus' presence encourage you toward peace and good cheer?

Chapter 17

For understanding
1. **Word Study: Glorify.** What is the biblical perspective on the "glory" of God? What are men doing when they "glorify" God? How is the glory of the eternal Son manifested in John's Gospel? What is Jesus asking the Father, then, to do?
2. **17:3.** What are the characteristics of our knowledge of God in his glory? According to Jeremiah, of what is personal knowledge of God the sign? On what Old Testament revelation is the New Testament revelation of the Trinity built?
3. **17:17.** For what purpose does Jesus ask the Father to "sanctify" the disciples? What is their task to be? What is the link between this "sanctification" and that of the Old Testament priesthood?
4. **17:23.** What kind of unity does Jesus desire? What is the source and pattern of the Church's unity?

For application
1. **17:3.** When does knowledge of "the only true God" begin? When, therefore, does eternal life begin?
2. **17:11.** How does the "family unity" that Jesus prayed for manifest itself in your parish? What kinds of groupings exist there? Where do you stand in relation to them? How are you working to see that Jesus' prayer is realized where you worship?
3. **17:14–17.** How does the saying "You can take the boy out of the country, but you can't take the country out of the boy" apply to your own relation with the *world*, on the one hand, and the *truth*, on the other? To which of the two do you—in your heart of hearts—belong? How do you know that?
4. **17:20–21.** Why does Jesus want all Christians to be in union with each other? What does our disunity do to the world's belief in Jesus? How does Jesus indicate that the issue of division should be addressed (see v. 23)?

Chapter 18

For understanding
1. **18:6.** What is one reason why those who come to arrest Jesus fall to the ground when he says, "I AM"?
2. **18:13.** Who is Annas? Why is he not functioning as high priest? What is his relationship to Caiaphas?
3. **18:15.** Who is the other disciple who follows Jesus with Peter? What tradition preserved by Eusebius would explain how this disciple came to know the high priest, the name of the high priest's slave, and the family of this slave?
4. **18:31.** What punishments is the Sanhedrin denied the right to administer to condemned criminals? What punishments do the Romans administer and to whom? Why is crucifixion virtually inevitable in Jesus' case?

For application
1. **18:4–11.** What does this passage suggest about who controls the situation? Why does he control it (v. 11)? How does your faith help you approach difficult or even dangerous situations?
2. **18:25–27.** Have you been in situations where you would have preferred that others not know you are a Christian or a Catholic? How did you deal with them? What did you think of your own conduct?
3. **18:37.** How does Jesus imply that his kingship is exercised? What do you think it means for one who is "of the truth" to "hear my voice"?

Chapter 19

For understanding
1.   **19:23.** What other vestment does the seamless tunic of Jesus recall? What is the implication? What allegorical meaning does St. Cyprian see in the seamless tunic?
2.   **19:26.** Why does Jesus address his Mother as "woman"? How does that address allude to Gen 3:15? In what way might John be regarded as an icon of every disciple when Jesus asks Mary to look upon him as her son? What assumption is being made regarding New Covenant family relationships?
3.   **19:34.** What is the literal significance of the blood and water from Jesus' side? How does the episode recall the story of the rock struck by Moses in the desert? How does Paul interpret it? What might the blood and water symbolize with respect to Christian sacraments?

For application
1.   **19:2-3.** What kind of suffering might the crown of thorns signify? What kinds of spiritual, mental, or emotional suffering have you endured? How have you handled it as a Christian?
2.   **19:7-9.** What is Pilate afraid of? How has superstition or dread of the unknown affected your religious life? Why does Jesus give Pilate no answer to his question?
3.   **19:26-27.** How would you characterize your filial relationship with Mary? Spiritually, how have you taken her into your own home?
4.   **19:28.** Compare this verse with v. 30. What kind of thirst other than the physical might Jesus have in mind?

Chapter 20

For understanding
1.   **20:7.** How do the linen shroud and the napkin provide corroborating evidence of the Resurrection?
2.   **20:20.** What point is Jesus making by showing the wounds in his hands and his side? How do we know that he carries these marks into heaven?
3.   **20:23.** When do the apostles carry out Jesus' mission of reconciling sinners? How is the authority to forgive or retain described elsewhere in the Gospels? According to the Council of Trent, when did Jesus institute the Sacrament of Reconciliation?
4.   **20:30-31.** What was John's purpose in writing his Gospel?

For application
1.   **20:13-14.** Recall some occasions in your life when you feared that God was distant from you but proved to be very near. How did you respond when you felt God was distant? How did you come to see his nearness?
2.   **20:19.** Have you ever locked the doors of your heart against the outside world (or against family or persons of other faiths) out of fear? What does Jesus' greeting of "Peace" do to allay the fear?
3.   **20:24-25.** Do you demand evidence from God before you will believe? Even if you do not demand it explicitly, what is there in your approach to God that might suggest you want him to prove himself?
4.   **20:28.** Under what circumstances are you liable to exclaim, "My Lord and my God!" along with Thomas? How might that prayer become more than a mere formula?

Chapter 21

For understanding

1. **21:9.** What is the significance behind the detail that the fire is a charcoal fire (compare to Jn 18:18)?
2. **21:11.** What might be the symbolism of the number of fish (153) that the disciples haul ashore?
3. **21:15-17.** Why does Peter reaffirm his love for Jesus three times? How might the different Greek verbs used for love in Jesus' question be significant (especially in the light of the single verb for love as friendship that Peter uses)? What does Jesus seem to want Peter to admit?
4. **21:15.** What does Jesus mean by telling Peter to "feed my lambs"? How does this square with Jesus' identity as the "Good Shepherd"? How does the First Vatican Council understand this passage?

For application

1. **21:7.** Why do you think it is Peter (who denied Jesus) who swims ashore rather than John (the disciple whom Jesus loves)? When have you been so eager to be with the Lord that you did something a bit foolish?
2. **21:15-17.** How do you love the Lord? How do you show it? Are you content just to be Jesus' friend, or do you want to go farther to a more sacrificial love?
3. **21:18-19.** Though Jesus' prediction applies specifically to Peter, it has a certain universality as well. How has God's call in your life led you to places, circumstances, or relationships you would rather have avoided? How has that been a "death" to self? How have you used it to glorify God?
4. **21:21-22.** When have you compared your talents, intellect, or spirituality to that of someone else? How has the comparison affected your relationship to that person or to God? What does Jesus tell you in this passage about making such comparisons?

BOOKS OF THE BIBLE

THE OLD TESTAMENT

Gen	Genesis
Ex	Exodus
Lev	Leviticus
Num	Numbers
Deut	Deuteronomy
Josh	Joshua
Judg	Judges
Ruth	Ruth
1 Sam	1 Samuel
2 Sam	2 Samuel
1 Kings	1 Kings
2 Kings	2 Kings
1 Chron	1 Chronicles
2 Chron	2 Chronicles
Ezra	Ezra
Neh	Nehemiah
Tob	Tobit
Jud	Judith
Esther	Esther
Job	Job
Ps	Psalms
Prov	Proverbs
Eccles	Ecclesiastes
Song	Song of Solomon
Wis	Wisdom
Sir	Sirach (Ecclesiasticus)
Is	Isaiah
Jer	Jeremiah
Lam	Lamentations
Bar	Baruch
Ezek	Ezekiel
Dan	Daniel
Hos	Hosea
Joel	Joel
Amos	Amos
Obad	Obadiah
Jon	Jonah
Mic	Micah
Nahum	Nahum
Hab	Habakkuk
Zeph	Zephaniah
Hag	Haggai
Zech	Zechariah
Mal	Malachi
1 Mac	Maccabees
2 Mac	2 Maccabees

THE NEW TESTAMENT

Mt	Matthew
Mk	Mark
Lk	Luke
Jn	John
Acts	Acts of the Apostles
Rom	Romans
1 Cor	1 Corinthians
2 Cor	2 Corinthians
Gal	Galatians
Eph	Ephesians
Phil	Philippians
Col	Colossians
1 Thess	1 Thessalonians
2 Thess	2 Thessalonians
1 Tim	1 Timothy
2 Tim	2 Timothy
Tit	Titus
Philem	Philemon
Heb	Hebrews
Jas	James
1 Pet	1 Peter
2 Pet	2 Peter
1 Jn	1 John
2 Jn	2 John
3 Jn	3 John
Jude	Jude
Rev	Revelation (Apocalypse)

NOTES

NOTES

NOTES

NOTES

NOTES